THE DIVINE SWORD OF EXU

AFRO-BRAZILIAN QUIMBANDA MAGIC RITUALS

CARLOS ANTONIO DE BOURBON-GALDIANO-MONTENEGRO

AMERICAN CANDOMBLE CHURCH PUBLICATIONS, LOS ANGELES, CALIFORNIA

THE DIVINE SWORD OF EXU

AFRO-BRAZILIAN QUIMBANDA MAGIC RITUALS

AMERICAN CANDOMBLE CHURCH PUBLICATIONS

P.O. BOX 881377

LOS ANGELES, CALIFORNIA 90009

<u>LEGAL DISCLAIMER</u>

No part of this book may be reproduced in any manner without written permission from the publisher or the author of this book. This book contains formulas that were used in the historical AFRO-BRAZILIAN religious practices of Quimbanda, Candomble, Macumba and Umbanda. The author and the publisher do not encourage any of the practices in this book nor do we assume any liabilities for presenting those formulas or any information in this book. The formulas are presented for curious only. Neither the author, Carlos Antonio De Bourbon-Galdiano-Montenegro nor the publisher, American Candomble Church assumes any responsibilities for the outcome of any of the spells, rituals or initiations in this book. We make no claims to any supernatural powers of these traditional initiation rituals. All inquiries or comments may be directed to the publisher. You must be at least 18 years of age or older to purchase this book or to purchase any of the supplies listed herein.

TABLE OF CONTENTS

FORMAL & INFORMAL RITUAL INSTRUCTIONS

The following sacred ceremonial ritual presented here in this book can be performed in a formal high magic context or in an informal high magic context.

If you will be performing the ritual of The Divine Sword of Exu formally then, follow the ritual instructions exactly as they are presented here in this sacred grimoire of Exu.

If you will be performing the Divine Sword of Exu informally, then the only ritual items that you will need is a white candle lighted, incense and a bell on your altar. The informal ritual of the Divine Sword of Exu does not need to use an actual consecrated sword. In the informal ritual, just place a chair directly in front of your altar and read the entire prayer.

This sacred ritual can also be performed directly in front of your spiritual altar (Boveda Espiritual).

For the informal ritual, just visualize the Divine Sword of Exu and cause the Holy Ritual into being.

SARAVA

The Divine Sword of Exu is a sacred book of occult knowledge to invoke the celestial powers of the Heavens to manifest here on Earth. This book is also called *The Sacred Grimoire of Exu*. A grimoire is a textbook of magic. The specific type of magic presented in this book is considered as ceremonial magic. Ceremonial magic, also referred to as high magic is a term used in the context of Hermeticism or Western Esotericism to encompass a wide variety of long, elaborate, and complex rituals of magic. *The Divine Sword of Exu* is a powerful magical invocation to summon the spirits of the *Seven Quimbanda Kingdoms* to triumph over one's enemies or to invoke these sacred divine powers for special spiritual requests and or desires. In order to see results from using this sacred ritual, you must follow the given ritual instructions exactly as they are prescribed and presented here in this sacred magical occult text.

MAGICAL OPERATIONS OF THE DIVINE SWORD OF EXU

The Divine Sword of Exu can be used to invoke and to summon the powerful entities of the Seven Quimbanda Kingdoms for various spiritual experiments such as "*Divine Justice*" and to triumph and to bring victory over any and all situations that are considered to be "just" and "righteous".

SACRED RITUAL LOCATIONS

The *Grand Ritual of the Divine Sword of Exu* should be performed in the sacred altar area of your temple. However, if you are not able to perform this sacred ritual in a designated sacred altar area, the places best fitted for exercising and accomplishing magical arts and operations are those which are concealed, removed, and separated from the habitations of men. Wherefore desolate and uninhabited regions are most appropriate, such as the borders of lakes, forests, dark and obscure places, old and deserted houses, whither rarely and scarce ever men do come, mountains, caves, caverns, grottos, gardens, orchards; but best of all are crossroads, and where four roads meet, during the depth and silence of night. But if you can't conveniently go unto any of these places, your house, and even your own bedroom or, indeed, any place, provided it has been purified and consecrated with the necessary ceremonies, will be found fit and convenient for the convocation and assembling of the spirits of the Seven Quimbanda Kingdoms. These magical occult arts or operations should be carried out at the prescribed time, but if there be no time specially appointed it will be always better to perform them at night, which is the most fit and proper time for the rituals and magical operations of Latin American necromancy; this is also a symbol that it is just and right to hide them from the sight of the foolish, the ignorant, and the profane. But when you have selected a place fitting, you may also perform these sacred experiments by day or by night. The ritual area should be spacious, clear, and bounded on all sides by hedges, shrubs, trees, or walls. Before commencing any operation of the magical occult arts, it should be spiritually cleansed thoroughly and render it neat and pure so that the spirits of the Seven Quimbanda Kingdoms will find it pleasing.

CONCERNING THE HOURS OF MAGICAL OPERATIONS

The *Grand Ritual of the Divine Sword of Exu* should be performed in the sacred altar area of your temple at night, which is the most fit and proper time for the operations of Latin American necromancy and to summon and invoke the spirits of the Seven Quimbanda Kingdoms. The best time to commence this ritual would be at 12 Midnight, at the start of a Full Moon. If starting this sacred ritual at 12 Midnight, it must be completed before the light of dawn or the ritual will be rendered without power and without effect.

THE PREPARATION OF THE ALTAR OF THE QUIMBANDA TRINITY

Ritually preparing the altar of the Quimbanda Trinity is an important aspect of performing this very powerful ritual. I have provided in the following pages various examples of how to correctly prepare an altar for the spirits of the Quimbanda Trinity. All Quimbanda altars should be set up facing the direction of the East. Altars can be set up in outside garden patios, balconies or in a designated ritual temple area in your home. Altars can also be temporaily set up for the purpose of performing this sacred ritual in remote locations such as the forest, fields, mountain, near the rivers or beaches. In the Quimbanda magico-religious tradition as practiced by the religious initiates of the *American Candomble Church*, having an altar set up in your temple or home is mandatory. An altar is any structure upon which offerings such as sacrifices and votive offerings are made for religious purposes, or some other sacred place where ceremonies take place. Altars are usually found at shrines, and they can be located in temples, churches and other places of worship. If you will be using the spells and sacred rituals from this book and from any other of my books written about the Quimbanda religious tradition you will need to first prepare an altar to their mysteries.

THE PREPARATION OF THE DIVINE SWORD OF EXU

In order to properly carry out the *Grand Ritual of the Divine Sword of Exu* it is necessary to ritually prepare it (ritual sword) to use it to invoke and summon the powers of the spirits of the Seven Quimbanda Kingdoms. Once the ritual to prepare the *Divine Sword of Exu* has been completed, it can be used in all important operations of the Quimbanda occult magical arts. The *Divine Sword of Exu* must be purchased or made new. The length of the *Divine Sword of Exu* must me at least 21 inches in length and sharp. The *Divine Sword of Exu* must be virgin in that it has not have been used in any prior magical rituals. The three spirit signatures of the Quimbanda Trinity must be inscribed on one side of the blade of the Divine Sword of Exu. The Quimbanda spirit signature which represents Nzambi must be inscribed on the other side of the blade of the *Divine Sword of Exu*. The spirit signatures on both sides of the *Divine Sword of Exu* can be permanently engraved or etched into and onto the blade. When the *Divine Sword of Exu* has been engraved with the sacred and holy signatures of the Quimbanda spirits, then it must be bathed and consecrated for ritual use. Bathe the *Divine Sword of Exu* in a liquid herbal mixture (***Amaci***) consisting of twenty-one sacred herbs of the Spirit Exu. Before bathing the *Divine Sword of Exu*, light a blessed white candle, do and say the following prayer:

Using your right hand, make the sign of the Quimbanda Trinity Cross over your body. The Quimbanda Trinity sign of the Cross is made by touching the hand sequentially to the forehead, lower chest or navel area, and right shoulder, then left shoulder and then placing your hands together in a praying position and then kissing your hands three times. This is how to say and do this: at the forehead, ***IN THE NAME OF NZAMBI***; at the naval, ***IN THE NAME OF EXU MAIORAL***; across to the right shoulder, ***IN THE NAME OF EXU REI***; across to the right left shoulder, ***IN THE NAME OF MARIA PADILLA REINA***; and finally to the center of your heart while placing your hands together in a praying position, ***SARAVA***; afterwards kiss your hands three times.

Take the Divine Sword of Exu and begin bathing it while reciting the following conjuration:

THE CONSECRATION OF THE DIVINE SWORD OF EXU

In the name of Nzambi, the God of the Heavens and the Earth, I conjure thee, O Divine Sword of Exu, by these names, EXU MAIORAL, EXU REI, MARIA PADILLA REINA the SEVEN GREATER QUIMBANDA KINGDOMS and the SEVEN LESSER QUIMBANDA KINGDOMS, that thou serve me for in the divine strength from the Heavens above and defence in all magical operations, against all mine enemies, visible and invisible. I conjure thee anew by the Holy and indivisible names of EXU REI DAS ENCRUZILHADAS and POMBA GIRA REINA DAS ENCRUZILHADAS – Sarava. I conjure thee anew by the Holy and indivisible names of EXU REI DOS SETE CRUZEIROS and POMBA GIA REINA DOS SETE CRUZEIROS – Sarava. I conjure thee anew by the Holy and indivisible names of EXU REI DAS MATAS and POMBA GIRA REINA DAS MATAS – Sarava. I conjure thee anew by the Holy and indivisible names of EXU REI KALUNGA and POMBA GIRA REINA KALUNGA – Sarava. I conjure thee anew by the Holy and indivisible names of EXU REI DAS ALMAS and POMBA GIRA DAS ALMAS – Sarava. I conjure thee anew by the Holy and indivisible names of EXU REI DAS LIRAS and POMBA GIRA DAS LIRAS – Sarava I conjure thee anew by the Holy and indivisible names of EXU REI DAS SETE PRAIAS and POMBA GIRA DAS SETE PRAIAS – Sarava By these sacred names and by all the other sacred Holy names of Heaven and Earth, I conjure thee, O Divine Sword of Exu that thou servest me for a protection in all adversities. – Sarava Nzambi, Most Holy, God of power and mighty, bless and consecrate this sacred and Divine Sword of Exu, that through your divine glory that it may obtain the necessary virtue, through thee, O most Holy Nzambi, whose Kingdom endureth unto the ages of the ages. Sarava

After having performed this ritual of consecration, wrap the Divine Sword of Exu up in a pure white, red or black silk cloth and then put it aside on the Quimbanda Trinity altar in a pure and clean place for use when required.

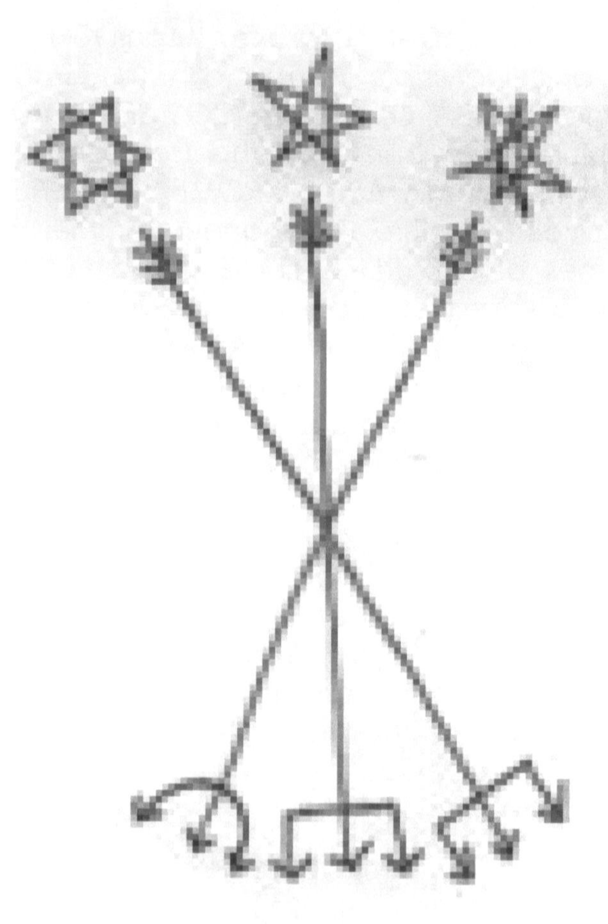

THE RITUAL PLACEMENT OF THE SIGILS ON THE DIVINE SWORD OF EXU (FRONT SIDE).

THE RITUAL PLACEMENT OF THE SIGILS ON THE DIVINE SWORD OF EXU (BACK SIDE). *In the following order, draw the Spirit Signatures of Exu Maioral, Exu Rei and Maria Padilla Reina.*

RITUAL CANDLES FOR THE DIVINE SWORD OF EXU

The ritual of the *Divine Sword of Exu* uses candles which must be ritually prepared in order to summon and invoke the powers of the spirits of the Quimbanda Trinity and the spirits of the Seven Greater Quimbanda Kingdoms and the Seven Lesser Quimbanda Kingdoms. Large altar pillar candles should be used in the conjuration ritual of the Divine Sword of Exu. These candles must be blessed and dressed and then consecrated before ritual use. After the altar pillar candles have been blessed, dressed and consecrated, they should be set into candle holders and then placed into their respective ritual ceremonial positions. To perform the ritual of the *Divine Sword of Exu* you will need all of the following number of altar pillar candles in the appropriate colors: 4 *Red Altar Pillar Candles*, 4 *Black Altar Pillar Candles*, 4 *White Altar Pillar Candles* and 1 *Silver Altar Pillar Candle*.

THE PREPARATION OF THE BLESSED RITUAL CANDLES

The altar pillar candles should all be ritually consecrated by preparing a sacred oil mixture consisting of the following magical items;

Blessed Olive Oil from a Catholic Church
Human Bone Powder from both Man and Woman
Rust Powder
Gold Powder
Silver Powder
Powdered Dirts from Seven Churches
Powdered Dirts from 21 Crossroads
Powdered Dirts from 21 Tombs of Men
Powdered Dirts from 21 Tombs of Women
Powdered Dirts from the Crossings
Powdered Dirts from the Forest & Mountains
Powdered Dirt from a Cemetery Gate
Powdered Dirt from a Funeral Parlor & Hospital
Powdered Dirt from a Bar
Powdered Dirt from the River
Powdered Dirt from the Beach

ALL OF THE POWDERED DIRTS USED IN THIS MAGICAL FORMULA REPRESENT THE SPIRITUAL FORCES OF THE SEVEN LESSER QUIMBANDA KINGDOMS.

THE CONSECRATION CONJURATION OF THE RITUAL CANDLES

As you are ritually preparing or dressing the altar pillar candles with the blessed oil and the other sacred ingredients, recite the following conjuration:

In the name of Nzambi, the God of the Heavens and the Earth, I exorcise thee, O creature of wax, that through the Holy name of God and the Quimbanda Trinity thou receive blessing, so that thou mayest be sanctified and be blessed, and obtain the virtue which I desire, through the most Holy name of Nzambi. I conjure thee through the powers of the Divine Sword of Exu, by these names, EXU MAIORAL, EXU REI, MARIA PADILLA REINA the SEVEN GREATER QUIMBANDA KINGDOMS and the SEVEN LESSER QUIMBANDA KINGDOMS, that thou serve me for in the divine strength from the Heavens above and defence in all magical operations, against all mine enemies, visible and invisible. Sarava

AFTER THE CANDLES HAVE BEEN CONSECRATED THEN PLACE THEM INTO RITUAL POSITION BEFORE YOU BEGIN THE RITUAL OF THE DIVINE SWORD OF EXU.

AN EXPLANATION OF THE SACRED SILVER CANDLE

The silver candle must always go inside of the Quimbanda magic circle to the left side of where you will be standing during the ritual. Along side of the silver candle you must place a large glass of fresh water next to it with a metal crucifix placed inside of the glass of water. After performing the ritual of the ***Divine Sword of Exu***, the water from the glass must be removed from the ritual area and poured at a crossroads far from your temple or residence where you will be performing the ritual. The crucifix must be removed just before pouring the water out from the glass. The water is placed within the magic Quimbanda circle to collect negative energy that may come during performing the ritual of the ***Divine Sword of Exu***.

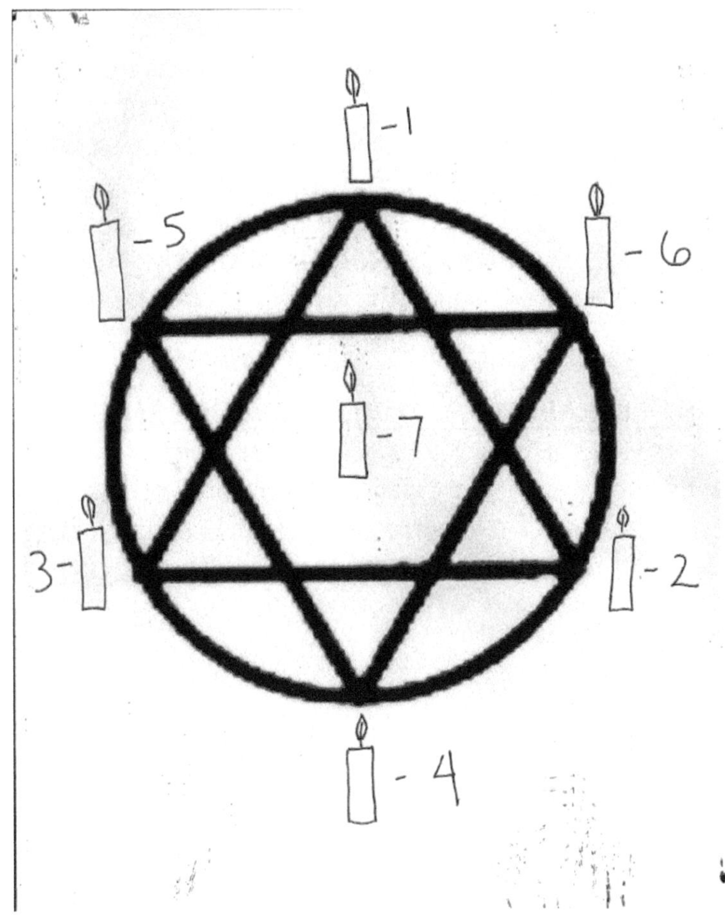

A DIAGRAM SHOWING THE RITUAL PLACEMENT OF THE BLESSED CANDLES.

THE EXORCISM OF INCENSE RITUAL

The ceremonial ritual area where you will be performing the sacred and holy ritual of the *Divine Sword of Exu* must be ritually cleansed using incense to remove any negative energy or obstructive vibrations which may affect the ritual from being fully realized. When using the ceremonial ritual incense to cleanse your sacred ritual area, take a brass bell and ring it seven times directly in front of the altar of the Holy Quimbanda Trinity and then ring it seven times in each of the four corners of the ritual area before passing the incense around the temple area to spiritually fumigate it.

THE PREPARATION OF THE RITUAL INCENSE

All of the following sacred ingredients should be pulverized into a fine powder using a stone motar and pestle. Prepare the ritual incense for the Divine Sword of Exu ritual using the following sacred herbs and magical ingredients;

CHURCH INCENSE RESIN
DRAGON'S BLOOD RESIN
ROSEMARY HERB (DRIED)
BASIL HERB (DRIED)
VENCEDOR HERB (DRIED)
SANDALWOOD POWDER
PATCHOULI HERB (DRIED)
ALLSPICE HERB (DRIED)
CLOVE HERB (DRIED)
HUMAN BONE POWDER FROM A MAN & A WOMAN

THE CEREMONIAL AREA FOR THE DIVINE SWORD RITUAL

When you wish to use the ritual incense, kindle a fire of fresh charcoal, in a ceremonial metal incense dish and the fire being lighted say the following "*Conjuration of the Sacred Fire*" before putting the ritually prepared powdered incense on it.

CONJURATION AND EXORCISM OF THE SACRED FIRE

I exorcise thee, O creature of fire, by Him through whom all things have been made, so that every kind of evil may retire from thee, and be unable to harm or deceive in any way, through the invocation of the Most High Creator of all. Sarava Bless, O Lord all powerful, and all merciful, this creature of fire, so that being blessed by thee, it may be for the honor and glory of thy most Holy name, so that it may work no hindrance or evil unto those who use it. Through thee, O Eternal and Almighty Lord, and through thy most Holy name. Sarava

CONJURATION OF THE RITUAL INCENSE FUMIGATION

This being done, place the ritually powdered incense on the hot charcoals and fumigate the ritual temple area. As you begin to prepare to fumigate the ceremonial area for the ritual of the *Divine Sword of Exu,* recite the following conjuration of the incense;

O Mighty God Nzambi who created all living things on Earth, bless these sacred ingredients so that they may receive strength, virtue, and power to attract the good spirits, and to banish and cause to retire all hostile forces. Through thee, O most Holy Nzambi, who livest and reignest unto the ages of the ages. Sarava

THE PREPARATION OF THE CEREMONIAL RITUAL AREA

Before you can begin this sacred ritual you must prepare your ceremonial ritual area that you will performing the prayer in. These are the things to do in order to have a successful magical ritual. Having chosen a place for preparing and constructing the magic circle of the Quimbanda Cross, and all things necessary being prepared for the perfection of the operations, set the prepared ritual candles in their respective locations located at each of the points of the Quimbanda Cross. The magic circle of the

Quimbanda Cross must be made directly in front of the altar of the Quimbanda Trinity. The dimensions of the magic circle of the Quimbanda Cross will be 7 feet round in diameter.

THE FORMATION OF THE MAGIC CIRCLE (QUIMBANDA CROSS)

Prepare your ritual space. Clean up and dust your altar and the area around it where you'll be creating your magic circle. Once the physical work is done, cleanse your space spiritually as well. After your altar has been set up correctly, you will need to draw the magic circle of the Quimbanda Cross on the ground using pemba (chalk) or white paint directly in front of the altar. The magic circle of the Quimbanda Cross should be made large enough for you to be able to stand in the center and on top of it. If there will be others participating in the ritual, make the circle of the Quimbanda Cross larger. After you have drawn the spirit signature of the Quimbanda Cross on the ground, draw a circle around it while moving in a clockwise direction, or in the direction of energetic creation when drawing the magic circle around the Quimbanda Cross. Make the circle only large enough to hold the members of the ritual and the ritual objects.

IF YOU WILL BE PERFORMING THIS RITUAL IN A FORMAL GROUP, THE MAGIC CIRCLE CAN BE ENLARGED TO 9 FEET ROUND IN DIAMETER OR 14 FEET ROUND IN DIAMETER.

QUIMBANDA CEREMONIAL RITUAL BATH

Before commencing on performing the sacred ritual of the *Divine Sword of Exu* you must always take a ritual bath to banish away any negative vibration from ones person. The Quimbanda Ceremonial Ritual Bath should be made from the fresh leaves of the sacred Ceiba Tree. The scientific name of the Ceiba Tree is *Ceiba Pentandra*. The Ceiba Tree is also known by religious practitioners of the Quimbanda tradition as the "spirit tree". The Ceiba Tree is believed topossess supernatural and spiritual powers and can fulfill wishes. The Ceiba Tree is venerated as being a powerful spiritual entity. It is also believed that the spirits of the ancestors rest beneath the shade of tree. In an ancient African myth, it is believed that the powerful Ancestor spirits used its large thorns which protrude on all sides of its trunk as a ladder to climb down from the Heavens to the Earth. The Ceiba Tree is also believed to have been the first tree created in the Garden of Eden. The Ceiba Tree is believed to be Nzambi's most sacred and favorite of all trees. It is also reccomended that you use Quimbanda Ritual Soap or African Black Soap (Dudu Osun), while bathing in the sacred ritual liquid bath of the Ceiba leaves. While bathing in the magical sacred ritual liquid bath of the Ceiba leaves recite the following conjuration;

O Most Holy Nzambi, you are the Lord of Lords and the King of the King of all Kings. I call upon thee, that this sacred bath may be salvation unto me, and that I may have my desire by thee. O Most Holy Nzambi who liveth and reigneth world without end. ***Sarava***

CEREMONIAL AND RITUAL CLOTHING

After taking your Quimbanda Ceremonial Ritual Bath and before commencing on performing the sacred ritual of the *Divine Sword of Exu*, place on yourself clean clothing. The appropriate ceremonial and ritual clothing can be any of the following;

All White Clothing
All Black Clothing
All Red Clothing
A Combination of White & Black Clothing
A Combination of Black & Red Clothing
A Combination of White, Black and Red Clothing
A Quimbanda Traditional Ritual Religious Ceremonial Robe

SACRED CEREMONIAL RITUAL JEWELRY

If you have been initiated into the sacred mysteries of the Quimbanda religious tradition, you can use and wear any of the sacred ceremonial ritual jewelry which was presented to you during the Quimbanda religious rites of passage initiations. If you have not been initiated into the sacred mysteries of the Quimbanda religious tradition then it would be appropriate to wear a silver religious medal or religious medallion of the Quimbanda Cross on a silver chain that has been blessed by a Quimbanda Priest. It is also appropriate to wear a ring made of silver with the sacred symbol of the Quimbanda Cross on the face of it. If using a ring of silver, it must be blessed by a Quimbanda Priest and the placed on the ring finger of the left hand.

THE DIVINE SWORD OF EXU

THE GRAND QUIMBANDA RITUAL TO INVOKE THE SPIRITSOF DIVINE JUSTICE

THE FORMATION OF THE MAGIC CIRCLE

Draw a large magic circle using white pemba (chalk) (3 to 7 feet round in diameter) in a clockwise position directly in front of the altar of the Quimbanda Trinity. Draw the spirit signature of the Quimbanda Cross inside of the magic circle. The spirit signature of the Quimbanda Cross should be made large enough so as the six points of the Quimbanda Cross touch the edges of the magic circle. Place the ritual colored altar pillar candles in their respective positions on the six points of the Quimbanda Cross. Place the red altar pillar candle on the altar of the Quimbanda Trinity in the position of the Spirit, Exu Maioral. The position is to the left side of the altar. Place the black altar pillar candle on the altar of the Quimbanda Trinity in the position of the Spirit, Exu Rei. The position is in the center of the altar. Place the white altar pillar candle on the altar of the Quimbanda Trinity in the position of the Spirit, Maria Padilla Reina. The position is to the left side of the altar. Place the silver altar pillar candle into the center of the magic circle of the Quimbanda Cross to the left side of where you will be standing to perfom the sacred ritual of the Divine Sword of Exu.

IF YOU HAVE THE ACTUAL SPIRIT MYSTERIES OF THE QUIMBANDA TRINITY ON YOUR ALTAR THEN PLACE THE CANDLES IN FRONT OF EACH SPIRIT NGANGA.

THE MAGIC CIRCLE OF THE QUIMBANDA TRINITY

Draw a large magic circle using red pemba (chalk) (12 inches round) in a clockwise position on the floor directly in front of the altar of the Quimbanda Trinity. The magic circle of Exu Maioral is to be placed on the left side of the altar of the Quimbanda Trinity. Draw the spirit signature of the Spirit, Exu Maioral inside of the magic circle. Place the red altar pillar candle into the center of the completed spirit circle of the Spirit, Exu Maioral. Draw a large magic circle using black pemba (chalk) (12 inches round) in a clockwise position on the floor directly in front of the altar of the Quimbanda Trinity. The magic circle of Exu Rei is to be placed in the center position of the altar of the Quimbanda Trinity. Draw the spirit signature of the Spirit, Exu Rei inside of the magic circle. Place the black altar pillar candle into the center of the completed spirit circle of the Spirit, Exu Rei.

Draw a large magic circle using white pemba (chalk) (12 inches round) in a clockwise position on the floor directly in front of the altar of the Quimbanda Trinity. The magic circle of Maria Padilla reina is to be placed on the right side of the altar of the Quimbanda Trinity. Draw the spirit signature of the Spirit, Maria Padilla Reina inside of the magic circle. Place the white altar pillar candle into the center of the completed spirit circle of the Spirit, Maria Padilla Reina.

THE RITUAL LIGHTING OF THE CANDLES OF THE HOLY TRINITY

Being fully prepared to begin the sacred ritual of the Divine Sword of Exu, stand in the center of the magic circle of the Quimbanda Cross. Begin the ritual by first lighting the red altar pillar candle in the center of the magic circle with the spirit signature of the Spirit, Exu Maioral. Then secondly light the black altar pillar candle of the Spirit, Exu Rei. Then lastly light the white altar pillar candle of the Spirit, Maria Padilla Reina.

THE CANDLES WHICH ARE PLACED ON TOP OF YOUR QUIMBANDA TRINITY ALTAR SHOULD BE ALWAYS LIGHTED TO GIVE THE SPIRITS STRENGTH TO LIGHT YOUR WAY.

THE LIGHTING OF THE SACRED CANDLES

Begin lighting each one of the consecrated altar pillar candles of the Quimbanda Cross of the magic circle. Light the candles in the sequential order as demonstrated in the following diagram drawing.

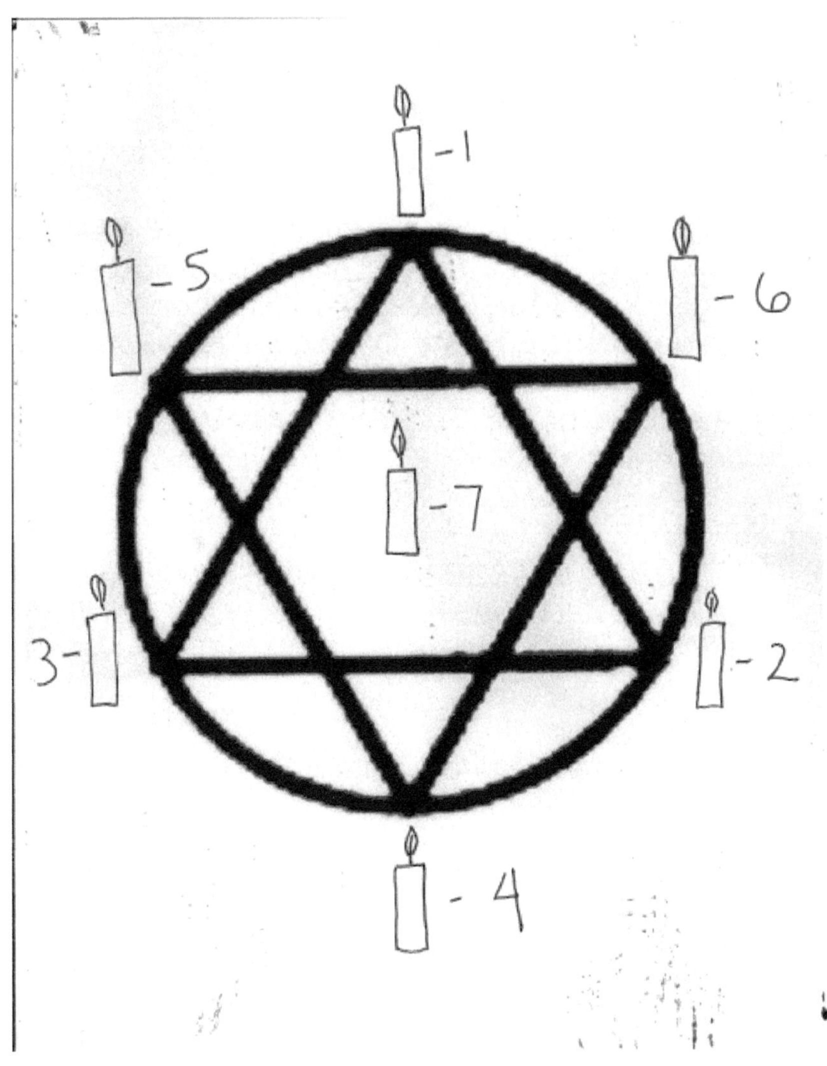

THE DIVINE RITUAL OF THE SACRED INVOCATIONS

Standing inside of the Quimbanda Cross directly in front of the Quimbanda altar facing the East do and say the following:

Using your right hand, make the sign of the Quimbanda Trinity Cross over your body. The Quimbanda Trinity sign of the Cross is made by touching the hand sequentially to the forehead, lower chest or navel area, and right shoulder, then left shoulder and then placing your hands together in a praying position and then kissing your hands three times. This is how to say and do this: at the forehead, ***IN THE NAME OF NZAMBI***; at the naval, ***IN THE NAME OF EXU MAIORAL***; across to the right shoulder, ***IN THE NAME OF EXU REI***; across to the right left shoulder, ***IN THE NAME OF MARIA PADILLA REINA***; and finally to the center of your heart while placing your hands together in a praying position, ***SARAVA***; afterwards kiss your hands three times.

Say the following:
BEFORE ME STANDS THE ARCHANGEL RAPHAEL. BEHIND ME STANDS THE ARCHANGEL GABRIEL. ON MY RIGHT HAND, THE ARCHANGEL MICHAEL AND ON MY LEFT HAND THE ARCHANGEL URIEL.

I invoke the Archangel Raphael, the Holy Guardian of the East and of the sacred element of Air.

Turn to face the West and do and say the following:
Using your right hand, make the sign of the Quimbanda Trinity Cross over your body. The Quimbanda Trinity sign of the Cross is made by touching the hand sequentially to the forehead, lower chest or navel area, and right shoulder, then left shoulder and then placing your hands together in a praying position and then kissing your hands three times. This is how to say and do this: at the forehead, ***IN THE NAME OF NZAMBI***; at the naval, ***IN THE NAME OF EXU MAIORAL***; across

to the right shoulder, ***IN THE NAME OF EXU REI***; across to the right left shoulder, ***IN THE NAME OF MARIA PADILLA REINA***; and finally to the center of your heart while placing your hands together in a praying position, ***SARAVA***; afterwards kiss your hands three times.

I invoke the Archangel Gabriel, the Holy Guardian of the West and of the sacred element of Water.

Turn to face the North and do and say the following:
Using your right hand, make the sign of the Quimbanda Trinity Cross over your body. The Quimbanda Trinity sign of the Cross is made by touching the hand sequentially to the forehead, lower chest or navel area, and right shoulder, then left shoulder and then placing your hands together in a praying position and then kissing your hands three times. This is how to say and do this: at the forehead, ***IN THE NAME OF NZAMBI***; at the naval, ***IN THE NAME OF EXU MAIORAL***; across to the right shoulder, ***IN THE NAME OF EXU REI***; across to the right left shoulder, ***IN THE NAME OF MARIA PADILLA REINA***; and finally to the center of your heart while placing your hands together in a praying position, ***SARAVA***; afterwards kiss your hands three times.

I invoke the Archangel Uriel, the Holy Guardian of the North and of the sacred element of Earth.

Turn to face the South and do and say the following:
Using your right hand, make the sign of the Quimbanda Trinity Cross over your body. The Quimbanda Trinity sign of the Cross is made by touching the hand sequentially to the forehead, lower chest or navel area, and right shoulder, then left shoulder and then placing your hands together in a praying position and then kissing your hands three times. This is how to say and do this: at the forehead, ***IN THE NAME OF NZAMBI***; at the naval, ***IN THE NAME OF EXU MAIORAL***; across to the right shoulder, ***IN THE NAME OF EXU REI***; across to the right left shoulder, ***IN THE NAME OF MARIA PADILLA REINA***;

and finally to the center of your heart while placing your hands together in a praying position, **SARAVA**; afterwards kiss your hands three times.

I invoke the Archangel Michael, the Holy Guardian of the South and of the sacred element of Fire.

Turn to face the East and do and say the following:
FOR AROUND MY BODY PROTECTED BY THE DIVINE LIGHT OF THE FLAMES OF THE QUIMBANDA TRINITY - SARAVA

Take up the consecrated Divine Sword of Exu using both of your hands and remove it from its sacred cloth on the Holy Quimbanda Trinity altar and kiss it three times. Kneel down in front of the Holy Quimbanda Trinity altar and hold the Divine Sword of Exu in both of your hands. Hold the Divine Sword of Exu in both of your hands, point it towards the Heavens saying the following invocation prayer:

Behold the great Divine Sword of Exu which commands the Seven Quimbanda Kingdoms. Behold the great Divine Sword of Exu which illuminates the Heavens. Behold the Divine Sword of the Exu which commands and turns the Universe. Behold the great Divine Sword of Exu which unlocks and opens the doors of Heaven and Earth. Behold the great Divine Sword of Exu which reveals the secrets and the mysteries of the Universe. Behold the great Divine Sword of Exu which Knights the heads of Kings with the Divine Crown of Glory. Behold the great Divine Sword of Exu which gives light in darkness. Behold the great Divine Sword of Exu which turns the day into night. Behold the great Divine Sword of Exu which turns the night into day. Behold the great Divine Sword of Exu which has the power to blind our enemies. Behold the great Divine Sword of Exu which has the power to bind our enemies. Behold the great Divine Sword of Exu which has the power to conquer our enemies. Behold the great Divine Sword of Exu which has the power to triumph over our enemies. Behold the Divine Sword of Exu which has the power to destroy and deliver us from our enemies. I, N.N., a humble servant of Nzambi do invoke the powers of the Divine Sword of Exu to deliver me from all tragedy and from all of my enemies. O Mighty and powerful Divine Sword of Exu, my enemies are your enemies. O Mighty and powerful Divine Sword of Exu, your enemies are my enemies. Holy, Holy, Holy God of power and might, Heaven and Earth are full of your glory, Hosanna in the Highest. Holy, Holy, Holy God of power and might, Heaven and Earth shall pass away, but your word will remain forever in the eternal light of the Quimbanda Trinity. By the power of the Lord of Heaven and the Divine Sword of Exu, I command this ritual into being. - SARAVA

Stand up in front of the Holy Quimbanda Trinity altar and hold the Sword of Exu in your right hand pointing it toward the altar of the Quimbanda Trinity and say the following:

O Lord God, Nzambi you are all powerful and all merciful, give and grant unto me thy grace, by blessing and consecrating this earth and this circle, which is here marked out with the most powerful and holy Cross of the Quimbanda Trinity. I conjure the most Holy Guardians of the Quimbanda Trinity, Exu Maioral, Exu Rei and Maria Padilla to bless and consecrate this holy circle. May Nzambi bless this place with all the virtues of Heaven, so that no obscene or unclean spirit may have the power to enter into this circle, or to annoy any person who is therein; though the Lord God Nzambi, who liveth eternally unto the ages of the ages. SARAVA

O Lord, hear my prayer, and let my cry come unto thee. O Lord God Almighty, who has reigned before the beginning of the Ages, and who by thine infinite wisdom, hast created the Heavens, the Earth, and the sea, and all that in them is, all that is visible, and all that is invisible by a single word; I praise thee, I bless thee, I adore thee, I glorify thee, and I pray thee now at the present time to be merciful unto me. O

God, the Father, all powerful and all merciful, who hast created all things, who knowest and conceivest them universally, and to whom nothing is hidden, nothing is impossible; I entreat thy grace for me and for thy servants, because thou seest and knowest well that we perform not this work to tempt thy strength and thy power as if in doubt thereof, but rather that we may know and understand the truth of all the hidden, I beseech thee to have the kindness to be favorable unto me; by thy splendour, thy magnificence, and thy holiness, and by thy holy, terrible, and ineffable name, at which the whole world doth tremble, and by the fear with which all creatures obey thee. Grant, O Lord, that we may become responsive unto thy grace, so that through it we may have a full confidence in and knowledge of thee, and that the spirits may discover themselves here in our presence, and that those which are gentle and peaceable may come unto us, so that they may be obedient unto thy commands, through thee, O most Holy Nzambi, whose Kingdom is an everlasting Kingdom, and whose empire endureth unto the ages of the ages. SARAVA

THE LESSER BANISHING RITUAL OF THE QUIMBANDA CROSS

Facing East towards the altar of the Quimbanda Trinity, with the *Divine Sword of Exu* in your right hand do the following: In silence, trace the *Lesser Banishing Ritual of the Quimbanda Cross* before you in the air using the *Divine Sword of Exu*. Turn towards the South with the *Divine Sword of Exu* in your right hand do the following: In silence, trace the *Lesser Banishing Ritual of the Quimbanda Cross* before you in the air using the *Divine Sword of Exu*. Turn towards the West with the *Divine Sword of Exu* in your right hand do the following: In silence, trace the *Lesser Banishing Ritual of the Quimbanda Cross* in the air using the *Divine Sword of Exu*. Turn towards the North with the *Divine Sword of Exu* in your right hand do the following: In silence, trance the *Lesser Banishing Ritual of the Quimbanda Cross* in the air using the *Divine Sword of Exu*. Turn towards the East facing the altar of the Quimbanda Trinity, with the *Divine Sword of Exu* in your right hand pointed towards the Heavens, say the following:

In the name of Nzambi, the Lord of Heaven - SARAVA
In the name of the Quimbanda Trinity, who govern the Heavens and the Earth - SARAVA
Exu by the Divine Sword of the King of Kings
I lay down my enemies at your feet - SARAVA
Exu by the Divine Sword of the King of Kings
I do bind my enemies in thy most sacred and holy name - SARAVA
Exu by the Divine Sword of the King of Kings
I do blind my enemies in thy most sacred and holy name - SARAVA
Exu by the Divine Sword of the King of Kings
I do destroy my enemies in thy most sacred and holy name - SARAVA
Exu by the Divine Sword of the King of Kings
Give me victory to triumph over my enemies - SARAVA
Exu by the Divine Sword of the King of Kings
Give me victory to defeat my enemies - SARAVA
Exu by the Divine Sword of the King of Kings
I wash my hands clean like Pontius Pilate - SARAVA

THE GREATER INVOKING RITUAL OF THE QUIMBANDA CROSS

Facing East towards the altar of the Quimbanda Trinity, with the *Divine Sword of Exu* in your right hand do the following: In silence, trace the *Greater Invoking Ritual of the Quimbanda Cross* before you in the air using the *Divine Sword of Exu*. Turn towards the South with the *Divine Sword of Exu* in your right hand do the following: In silence, trace the *Greater Invoking Ritual of the Quimbanda Cross* before you in the air using the *Divine Sword of Exu*. Turn towards the West with the *Divine Sword of Exu* in your right hand do the following: In silence, trace the *Greater Invoking Ritual of the Quimbanda Cross* in the air using the *Divine Sword of Exu*. Turn towards the North with the *Divine Sword of Exu* in your right hand do the following: In silence, trance the *Greater Invoking Ritual of the Quimbanda Cross* in the air using the *Divine Sword of Exu*. Turn towards the East facing the altar of the Quimbanda Trinity, with the *Divine Sword of Exu* in your right hand pointed towards the Heavens, say the following:

In the name of Nzambi, The God of the Heavens and the Earth – Sarava. In the name of Exu Maioral - Sarava
In the name of Exu Rei - Sarava
In the name of Maria Padilla Reina - Sarava
In the name of the Quimbanda Trinity - Sarava
In the name of the Seven Quimbanda Kingdoms - Sarava
In the name of my ancestors who are kneeling at your feet in light, Nzambi- Sarava
By the Divine power of the Quimbanda Trinity, I do summon your Spirit, O Mighty Nzambi to come forth to give life to this sacred ritual and cause it into being. Sarava

THE SACRED CONJURATION OF THE NAMES OF GOD

Before reciting the following conjuration do the following ritual: Kneel down on your left knee in front of the altar of the Holy Quimbanda Trinity facing East and then ring a brass bell three times using your right hand. After ringing the bell three times, stand up with the Divine Sword of Exu in your right hand pointed towards the Holy Quimbanda Trinity altar and towards the Heavens and then say the following ritual conjuration:

By the power of the Divine Sword of Exu, I do invoke the celestial mysteries of Heaven. O Mighty God, Nzambi who has created all things in the Heavens and the Earth, through your Divine power, By the divine celestial chain which binds the Heavens and the Earth, I invoke thee, O Mighty Nzambi. O Mighty God, Nzambi who has created all things in the Heavens and the Earth and has given unto me the wisdom of discernment to understand the good and the evil; through your Divine power, I do invoke the powers of the Divine Sword of Exu through thy sacred and Holy Names of praise. In the name of the Quimbanda Trinity and the Seven Holy Quimbanda Kingdoms – Sarava. By the Divine Right of Kings, I summon and invoke the sacred mysteries of the Great Divine Creator and the Divine Sword of Exu.

Nzambi - Let us pray:

In the name of ***Nzambi Mpungo****, the God of the Heavens.*
Lord Hear Our Prayer - Sarava

In the name of ***Nzambi Ntoto****, the God who walked and touched the Earth.*

Lord Hear Our Prayer - Sarava

In the name of all of your sacred praise names that you are known in the great universe - Sarava.

O mighty and powerful Nzambi, you are the Alpha and the Omega and from your sacred praise names let light conqueor all darkness. – Sarava.

O Spirits of the Quimbanda Trinity, I, N.N., conjure this sacred ritual into being by the power, wisdom, and virtue of the Spirit of God, by the divine knowledge of God, by the infinite mercy of God, by the strength of God, by the greatness of God, by the unity of God and by all of the holy names of God which are the root, trunk, source, and origin of the Divine Seven Quimbanda Kingdoms, whence they all draw their life and their virtue, which Adam and Lilith having invoked, they acquired the knowledge of all created things.

THE CONJURATIONS OF THE FIRST GREATER KINGDOM

Before reciting the following conjuration do the following ritual: Kneel down on your left knee in front of the altar of the Holy Quimbanda Trinity facing East and then ring a brass bell three times using your right hand. After ringing the bell three times, stand up with the Divine Sword of Exu in your right hand pointed towards the Holy Quimbanda Trinity altar and towards the Heavens and then say the following ritual conjuration:

With the *Divine Sword of Exu* in your right hand, make the sign of the Quimbanda Trinity Cross over your body. The Quimbanda Trinity sign of the Cross is made by touching the hand sequentially to the forehead, lower chest or navel area, and right shoulder, then left shoulder and then placing your hands together in a praying position around the handle of the *Divine Sword of Exu* and then kissing the *Divine Sword of Exu* three times. This is how to say and do this: present the *Divine Sword of Exu* at the forehead, ***IN THE NAME OF NZAMBI***; present the *Divine Sword of Exu* at the naval, ***IN THE NAME OF EXU MAIORAL***; present the *Divine Sword of Exu* across to the right shoulder, ***IN THE NAME OF EXU REI***; present the *Divine Sword of Exu* across to the right left shoulder, ***IN THE NAME OF MARIA PADILLA REINA***; and finally present the *Divine Sword of Exu* to the center of your heart in a praying position, ***SARAVA***; afterwards kiss your hands that are wraped around the handle of the *Divine Sword of Exu* three times.

After blessing yourself with the Divine Sword of Exu recite the following invocation:

Blessed are you, O Lord Nzambi, for you created the Heavens, the Earth and the Seven Quimbanda Kingdoms to protect and to serve all of mankind. Blessed are you, O Lord Nzambi, for you brought down from the Heavens the *Divine Sword of Exu* to triumph over and to conquer our enemies.

May we worship you and give thanks to thee O powerful King of the Heavens and all your divine glory. Sarava

After reciting the sacred invocation, do the following: Stand up facing the altar of the Quimbanda Trinity in the East and hold the Divine Sword of Exu in your right hand and point it towards the altar and towards the Heavens.

Turn towards the East facing the altar of the Quimbanda Trinity, with the *Divine Sword of Exu* in your right hand pointed towards the Heavens, say the following Conjurations of the First Greater Quimbanda Kingdom;

IN THE NAME OF NZAMBI, THE GOD OF THE HEAVENS AND THE EARTH - SARAVA
IN THE NAME OF EXU MAIORAL - SARAVA
IN THE NAME OF EXU REI - SARAVA
IN THE NAME OF MARIA PADILLA REINA - SARAVA
IN THE NAME OF THE QUIMBANDA TRINITY - SARAVA
INVOCATION RITUAL TO SUMMON THE DEITY, EXU MAIORAL
IN THE NAME OF NZAMBI, THE GOD OF THE HEAVENS AND THE EARTH - SARAVA
IN THE NAME OF EXU MAIORAL, DIVINE KING, SPIRIT AND EMPEROR OF THE FIRST GREATER QUIMBANDA KINGDOM, I, N.N., INVOKE THY SACRED AND DIVINE POWERS OF THE SEVEN GREATER QUIMBANDA KINGDOMS. IN THE NAME OF EXU MAIORAL, I, N.N., INVOKE THE POWERS THAT BE UNDER YOUR DIVINE COMMAND AND TO HEAR MY REQUEST OF DIVINE JUSTICE BY THE SWORD OF EXU.

THE CONJURATION OF THE HOLY ARCHANGEL METATRON

Before reciting the following conjuration do the following ritual: Ring a brass bell three times using your right hand. After ringing the bell three times, with the Divine Sword of Exu in your right hand pointed towards the Holy Quimbanda Trinity altar and towards the Heavens and then say the following ritual conjuration:

I, N.N., a servant of Nzambi, call upon the Archangel Metatron and conjure thee by the power of the Divine Sword of Exu Maioral, and the Sacred Fire of God which which thou has been granted to light and transform the world of the living and the dead. I conjure thee O Mighty Archangel Metatron, the Seven Holy Archangels and the Most Holy Quimbanda Trinity to manifest here to me and take my command. O Mighty Archangel Metatron, Chancellor of Heaven and Divine King of the Archangels by the power of the sacred Fire of God all bow down to thee. O Mighty Archangel Metatron, you are the great Fire of God which illuminated and gave the Earth light and life. O Mighty Archangel Metatron by the supreme power of the great Guardians of the Seven Quimbanda Kingdoms who govern over the celestial mysteries of the divine universe and govern over the Heavens. I, N.N.., a servant of Nzambi do summon you and command you to come forth and hear my request. I, N.N.., a servant of Nzambi do summon you and command you to come forth and grant my request. O Great Angelic King by your will and authority of Nzambi, the God Most High, I summon you to command the sacred legions of thy Holy Seven Archangels, the Archangel Michael, the Archangel Raphael, the Archangel Gabriel, the Archangel Uriel, the Archangel Anael, the Archangel Zerachiel and the Archangel Raziel to take your command by the power of the Divine Sword of Exu ye shall be commanded to come forth and grant my request, SARAVA

THE CONJURATION OF THE HOLY ARCHANGEL GABRIEL

Before reciting the following conjuration do the following ritual: Ring a brass bell three times using your right hand. After ringing the bell three times, with the Divine Sword of Exu in your right hand pointed towards the Holy Quimbanda Trinity altar and towards the Heavens and then say the following ritual conjuration:

I, N.N., a servant of Nzambi, call upon the Archangel Gabriel, O Holy Heavenly Host and Divine Guardian of the Mysteries of the Constellations, hear my prayer. O Mighty and powerful Archangel Gabriel, to you I call and to you I conjure thee by the power of the Divine Sword of Exu, the fire of the Archangel Metatron, and the Most Holy Quimbanda Trinity to manifest here to me and take my command. By the supreme power of the great Guardians of the Seven Quimbanda Kingdoms who govern over the celestial mysteries of the divine universe and govern over the Heavens. I, N.N.., a servant of Nzambi do summon you and command you to come forth and hear my request. I, N.N.., a servant of Nzambi do summon you and command you to come forth and grant my request. By the power of the Divine Sword of Exu ye shall be commanded to come forth and grant my request, SARAVA

THE CONJURATION OF THE HOLY ARCHANGEL RAPHAEL

Before reciting the following conjuration do the following ritual: Ring a brass bell three times using your right hand. After ringing the bell three times, with the Divine Sword of Exu in your right hand pointed towards the Holy Quimbanda Trinity altar and towards the Heavens and then say the following ritual conjuration:

I, N.N., a servant of Nzambi, call upon the Archangel Raphael, O Holy Heavenly Host and Divine Guardian of the Mysteries of the Constellations, hear my prayer. O Mighty and powerful Archangel Raphael, to you I call and to you I conjure thee by the power of the Divine Sword of Exu, the fire of the Archangel Metatron, and the Most Holy Quimbanda Trinity to manifest here to me and take my command. By the supreme power of the great Guardians of the Seven Quimbanda Kingdoms who govern over the celestial mysteries of the divine universe and govern over the Heavens. I, N.N.., a servant of Nzambi do summon you and command you to come forth and hear my request. I, N.N.., a servant of Nzambi do summon you and command you to come forth and grant my request. By the power of the Divine Sword of Exu ye shall be commanded to come forth and grant my request, SARAVA

THE SACRED CONJURATION OF THE HOLY ARCHANGEL ANAEL

Before reciting the following conjuration do the following ritual: Ring a brass bell three times using your right hand. After ringing the bell three times, with the Divine Sword of Exu in your right hand pointed towards the Holy Quimbanda Trinity altar and towards the Heavens and then say the following ritual conjuration;

I, N.N., a servant of Nzambi, call upon the Archangel Anael, O Holy Heavenly Host and Divine Guardian of the Mysteries of the Constellations, hear my prayer. O Mighty and powerful Archangel Anael, to you I call and to you I conjure thee by the power of the Divine Sword of Exu, the fire of the Archangel Metatron, and the Most Holy Quimbanda Trinity to manifest here to me and take my command. By the supreme power of the great Guardians of the Seven Quimbanda Kingdoms who govern over the celestial mysteries of the divine universe and govern over the Heavens. I, N.N.., a servant of Nzambi do summon you and command you to come forth and hear my request. I, N.N.., a servant of Nzambi do summon you and command you to come forth and grant my request. By the power of the Divine Sword of Exu ye shall be commanded to come forth and grant my request, SARAVA

THE CONJURATION OF THE HOLY ARCHANGEL MICHAEL

Before reciting the following conjuration do the following ritual: Ring a brass bell three times using your right hand. After ringing the bell three times, with the Divine Sword of Exu in your right hand pointed towards the Holy Quimbanda Trinity altar and towards the Heavens and then say the following ritual conjuration:

I, N.N., a servant of Nzambi, call upon the Archangel Michael, O Holy Heavenly Host and Divine Guardian of the Mysteries of the Constellations, hear my prayer. O Mighty and powerful Archangel Michael, to you I call and to you I conjure thee by the power of the Divine Sword of Exu, the fire of the Archangel Metatron, and the Most Holy Quimbanda Trinity to manifest here to me and take my command. By the supreme power of the great Guardians of the Seven Quimbanda Kingdoms who govern over the celestial mysteries of the divine universe and govern over the Heavens. I, N.N.., a servant of Nzambi do summon you and command you to come forth and hear my request. I, N.N.., a servant of Nzambi do summon you and command you to come forth and grant my request. By the power of the Divine Sword of Exu ye shall be commanded to come forth and grant my request, SARAVA

THE SACRED CONJURATION OF THE HOLY ARCHANGEL RAZIEL

Before reciting the following conjuration do the following ritual: Ring a brass bell three times using your right hand. After ringing the bell three times, with the Divine Sword of Exu in your right hand pointed towards the Holy Quimbanda Trinity altar and towards the Heavens and then say the following ritual conjuration:

I, N.N., a servant of Nzambi, call upon the Archangel Raziel, O Holy Heavenly Host and Divine Guardian of the Mysteries of the Constellations, hear my prayer. O Mighty and powerful Archangel Raziel, to you I call and to you I conjure thee by the power of the Divine Sword of Exu, the fire of the Archangel Metatron, and the Most Holy Quimbanda Trinity to manifest here to me and take my command. By the supreme power of the great Guardians of the Seven Quimbanda Kingdoms who govern over the celestial mysteries of the divine universe and govern over the Heavens. I, N.N.., a servant of Nzambi do summon you and command you to come forth and hear my request. I, N.N.., a servant of Nzambi do summon you and command you to come forth and grant my request. By the power of the Divine Sword of Exu ye shall be commanded to come forth and grant my request, SARAVA

THE CONJURATION OF THE HOLY ARCHANGEL ZERACHIEL

Before reciting the following conjuration do the following ritual: Ring a brass bell three times using your right hand. After ringing the bell three times, with the Divine Sword of Exu in your right hand pointed towards the Holy Quimbanda Trinity altar and towards the Heavens and then say the following ritual conjuration:

I, N.N., a servant of Nzambi, call upon the Archangel Zerachiel, O Holy Heavenly Host and Divine Guardian of the Mysteries of the Constellations, hear my prayer. O Mighty and powerful Archangel Zerachiel, to you I call and to you I conjure thee by the power of the Divine Sword of Exu, the fire of the Archangel Metatron, and the Most Holy Quimbanda Trinity to manifest here to me and take my command. By the supreme power of the great Guardians of the Seven Quimbanda Kingdoms who govern over the celestial mysteries of the divine universe and govern over the Heavens. I, N.N.., a servant of Nzambi do summon you and command you to come forth and hear my request. I, N.N.., a servant of Nzambi do summon you and command you to come forth and grant my request. By the power of the Divine Sword of Exu ye shall be commanded to come forth and grant my request, SARAVA

THE SACRED CONJURATION OF THE HOLY ARCHANGEL URIEL

Before reciting the following conjuration do the following ritual: Ring a brass bell three times using your right hand. After ringing the bell three times, with the Divine Sword of Exu in your right hand pointed towards the Holy Quimbanda Trinity altar and towards the Heavens and then say the following ritual conjuration:

I, N.N., a servant of Nzambi, call upon the Archangel Uriel, O Holy Heavenly Host and Divine Guardian of the Mysteries of the Constellations, hear my prayer. O Mighty and powerful Archangel Uriel, to you I call and to you I conjure thee by the power of the Divine Sword of Exu, the fire of the Archangel Metatron, and the Most Holy Quimbanda Trinity to manifest here to me and take my command. By the supreme power of the great Guardians of the Seven Quimbanda Kingdoms who govern over the celestial mysteries of the divine universe and govern over the Heavens. I, N.N.., a servant of Nzambi do summon you and command you to come forth and hear my request. I, N.N.., a servant of Nzambi do summon you and command you to come forth and grant my request. By the power of the Divine Sword of Exu ye shall be commanded to come forth and grant my request, SARAVA

CONJURATIONS OF THE SEVENTY-TWO SPIRITS OF EXU

Before reciting the following conjuration do the following ritual: Ring a brass bell three times using your right hand. After ringing the bell three times, with the Divine Sword of Exu in your right hand pointed towards the Holy Quimbanda Trinity altar and towards the Heavens and then say the following ritual conjuration:

THE SACRED CONJURATION OF EXU BAEL

I, N.N., a servant of Nzambi, call upon Exu Bael, and conjure thee by the power of Exu Maioral and the Divine Sword of Exu, the fire of the Archangel Metatron, the Seven Holy Archangels and the Most Holy Quimbanda Trinity to manifest here to me and take my command.

THE SACRED CONJURATION OF EXU AGARES

I, N.N., a servant of Nzambi, call upon Exu Agares, and conjure thee by the power of Exu Maioral and the Divine Sword of Exu, the fire of the Archangel Metatron, the Seven Holy Archangels and the Most Holy Quimbanda Trinity to manifest here to me and take my command.

THE SACRED CONJURATION OF EXU VASSAGE

I, N.N., a servant of Nzambi, call upon Exu Vassage, and conjure thee by the power of Exu Maioral and the Divine Sword of Exu, the fire of the Archangel Metatron, the Seven Holy Archangels and the Most Holy Quimbanda Trinity to manifest here to me and take my command.

THE SACRED CONJURATION OF EXU SAMIGINA

I, N.N., a servant of Nzambi, call upon Exu Samigina, and conjure thee by the power of Exu Maioral and the Divine Sword of Exu, the fire of the Archangel Metatron, the Seven Holy Archangels and the Most Holy Quimbanda Trinity to manifest here to me and take my command.

THE SACRED CONJURATION OF EXU MARBAS

I, N.N., a servant of Nzambi, call upon Exu Marbas, and conjure thee by the power of Exu Maioral and the Divine Sword of Exu, the fire of the Archangel Metatron, the Seven Holy Archangels and the Most Holy Quimbanda Trinity to manifest here to me and take my command.

THE SACRED CONJURATION OF EXU VALEFOR

I, N.N., a servant of Nzambi, call upon Exu Valefor, and conjure thee by the power of Exu Maioral and the Divine Sword of Exu, the fire of the Archangel Metatron, the Seven Holy Archangels and the Most Holy Quimbanda Trinity to manifest here to me and take my command.

THE SACRED CONJURATION OF EXU AMON

I, N.N., a servant of Nzambi, call upon Exu Amon, and conjure thee by the power of Exu Maioral and the Divine Sword of Exu, the fire of the Archangel Metatron, the Seven Holy Archangels and the Most Holy Quimbanda Trinity to manifest here to me and take my command.

THE SACRED CONJURATION OF EXU BARBATOS

I, N.N., a servant of Nzambi, call upon Exu Barbatos, and conjure thee by the power of Exu Maioral and the Divine Sword of Exu, the fire of the Archangel Metatron, the Seven Holy Archangels and the Most Holy Quimbanda Trinity to manifest here to me and take my command.

THE SACRED CONJURATION OF EXU PAIMON

I, N.N., a servant of Nzambi, call upon Exu Paimon, and conjure thee by the power of Exu Maioral and the Divine Sword of Exu, the fire of the Archangel Metatron, the Seven Holy Archangels and the Most Holy Quimbanda Trinity to manifest here to me and take my command.

THE SACRED CONJURATION OF EXU BUER

I, N.N., a servant of Nzambi, call upon Exu Buer, and conjure thee by the power of Exu Maioral and the Divine Sword of Exu, the fire of the Archangel Metatron, the Seven Holy Archangels and the Most Holy Quimbanda Trinity to manifest here to me and take my command.

THE SACRED CONJURATION OF EXU GUSION

I, N.N., a servant of Nzambi, call upon Exu Gusion, and conjure thee by the power of Exu Maioral and the Divine Sword of Exu, the fire of the Archangel Metatron, the Seven Holy Archangels and the Most Holy Quimbanda Trinity to manifest here to me and take my command.

THE SACRED CONJURATION OF EXU SITRI

I, N.N., a servant of Nzambi, call upon Exu Sitri, and conjure thee by the power of Exu Maioral and the Divine Sword of Exu, the fire of the Archangel Metatron, the Seven Holy Archangels and the Most Holy Quimbanda Trinity to manifest here to me and take my command.

THE SACRED CONJURATION OF EXU BELETH

I, N.N., a servant of Nzambi, call upon Exu Beleth, and conjure thee by the power of Exu Maioral and the Divine Sword of Exu, the fire of the Archangel Metatron, the Seven Holy Archangels and the Most Holy Quimbanda Trinity to manifest here to me and take my command.

THE SACRED CONJURATION OF EXU LERAJE

I, N.N., a servant of Nzambi, call upon Exu Leraje, and conjure thee by the power of Exu Maioral and the Divine Sword of Exu, the fire of the Archangel Metatron, the Seven Holy Archangels and the Most Holy Quimbanda Trinity to manifest here to me and take my command.

THE SACRED CONJURATION OF EXU ELIGOS

I, N.N., a servant of Nzambi, call upon Exu Eligos, and conjure thee by the power of Exu Maioral and the Divine Sword of Exu, the fire of the Archangel Metatron, the Seven Holy Archangels and the Most Holy Quimbanda Trinity to manifest here to me and take my command.

THE SACRED CONJURATION OF EXU ZEPAR

I, N.N., a servant of Nzambi, call upon Exu Zepar, and conjure thee by the power of Exu Maioral and the Divine Sword of Exu, the fire of the Archangel Metatron, the Seven Holy Archangels and the Most Holy Quimbanda Trinity to manifest here to me and take my command.

THE SACRED CONJURATION OF EXU BOTIS

I, N.N., a servant of Nzambi, call upon Exu Botis, and conjure thee by the power of Exu Maioral and the Divine Sword of Exu, the fire of the Archangel Metatron, the Seven Holy Archangels and the Most Holy Quimbanda Trinity to manifest here to me and take my command.

THE SACRED CONJURATION OF EXU BATHIN

I, N.N., a servant of Nzambi, call upon Exu Bathin, and conjure thee by the power of Exu Maioral and the Divine Sword of Exu, the fire of the Archangel Metatron, the Seven Holy Archangels and the Most Holy Quimbanda Trinity to manifest here to me and take my command.

THE SACRED CONJURATION OF EXU SALLOS

I, N.N., a servant of Nzambi, call upon Exu Sellos, and conjure thee by the power of Exu Maioral and the Divine Sword of Exu, the fire of the Archangel Metatron, the Seven Holy Archangels and the Most Holy Quimbanda Trinity to manifest here to me and take my command.

THE SACRED CONJURATION OF EXU PURSON

I, N.N., a servant of Nzambi, call upon Exu Purson, and conjure thee by the power of Exu Maioral and the Divine Sword of Exu, the fire of the Archangel Metatron, the Seven Holy Archangels and the Most Holy Quimbanda Trinity to manifest here to me and take my command.

THE SACRED CONJURATION OF EXU MARAX

I, N.N., a servant of Nzambi, call upon Exu Marax, and conjure thee by the power of Exu Maioral and the Divine Sword of Exu, the fire of the Archangel Metatron, the Seven Holy Archangels and the Most Holy Quimbanda Trinity to manifest here to me and take my command.

THE SACRED CONJURATION OF EXU IPOS

I, N.N., a servant of Nzambi, call upon Exu Ipos, and conjure thee by the power of Exu Maioral and the Divine Sword of Exu, the fire of the Archangel Metatron, the Seven Holy Archangels and the Most Holy Quimbanda Trinity to manifest here to me and take my command.

THE SACRED CONJURATION OF EXU AIM

I, N.N., a servant of Nzambi, call upon Exu Aim, and conjure thee by the power of Exu Maioral and the Divine Sword of Exu, the fire of the Archangel Metatron, the Seven Holy Archangels and the Most Holy Quimbanda Trinity to manifest here to me and take my command.

THE SACRED CONJURATION OF EXU NABERIUS

I, N.N., a servant of Nzambi, call upon Exu Naberius, and conjure thee by the power of Exu Maioral and the Divine Sword of Exu, the fire of the Archangel Metatron, the Seven Holy Archangels and the Most Holy Quimbanda Trinity to manifest here to me and take my command.

THE SACRED CONJURATION OF EXU GLASYA-LABOLAS

I, N.N., a servant of Nzambi, call upon Exu Glasya-Labolas, and conjure thee by the power of Exu Maioral and the Divine Sword of Exu, the fire of the Archangel Metatron, the Seven Holy Archangels and the Most Holy Quimbanda Trinity to manifest here to me and take my command.

THE SACRED CONJURATION OF EXU BUNE

I, N.N., a servant of Nzambi, call upon Exu Bune, and conjure thee by the power of Exu Maioral and the Divine Sword of Exu, the fire of the Archangel Metatron, the Seven Holy Archangels and the Most Holy Quimbanda Trinity to manifest here to me and take my command.

THE SACRED CONJURATION OF EXU RONOVE

I, N.N., a servant of Nzambi, call upon Exu Ronove, and conjure thee by the power of Exu Maioral and the Divine Sword of Exu, the fire of the Archangel Metatron, the Seven Holy Archangels and the Most Holy Quimbanda Trinity to manifest here to me and take my command.

THE SACRED CONJURATION OF EXU BERITH

I, N.N., a servant of Nzambi, call upon Exu Berith, and conjure thee by the power of Exu Maioral and the Divine Sword of Exu, the fire of the Archangel Metatron, the Seven Holy Archangels and the Most Holy Quimbanda Trinity to manifest here to me and take my command.

THE SACRED CONJURATION OF EXU ASTAROTH

I, N.N., a servant of Nzambi, call upon Exu Astaroth, and conjure thee by the power of Exu Maioral and the Divine Sword of Exu, the fire of the Archangel Metatron, the Seven Holy Archangels and the Most Holy Quimbanda Trinity to manifest here to me and take my command.

THE SACRED CONJURATION OF EXU FORNEUS

I, N.N., a servant of Nzambi, call upon Exu Forneus, and conjure thee by the power of Exu Maioral and the Divine Sword of Exu, the fire of the Archangel Metatron, the Seven Holy Archangels and the Most Holy Quimbanda Trinity to manifest here to me and take my command.

THE SACRED CONJURATION OF EXU FORAS

I, N.N., a servant of Nzambi, call upon Exu Foras, and conjure thee by the power of Exu Maioral and the Divine Sword of Exu, the fire of the Archangel Metatron, the Seven Holy Archangels and the Most Holy Quimbanda Trinity to manifest here to me and take my command.

THE SACRED CONJURATION OF EXU ASMODAY

I, N.N., a servant of Nzambi, call upon Exu Asmoday, and conjure thee by the power of Exu Maioral and the Divine Sword of Exu, the fire of the Archangel Metatron, the Seven Holy Archangels and the Most Holy Quimbanda Trinity to manifest here to me and take my command.

THE SACRED CONJURATION OF EXU GAAP

I, N.N., a servant of Nzambi, call upon Exu Gaap, and conjure thee by the power of Exu Maioral and the Divine Sword of Exu, the fire of the Archangel Metatron, the Seven Holy Archangels and the Most Holy Quimbanda Trinity to manifest here to me and take my command.

THE SACRED CONJURATION OF EXU FURFUR

I, N.N., a servant of Nzambi, call upon Exu Furfur, and conjure theeby the power of Exu Maioral and the Divine Sword of Exu, the fire of the Archangel Metatron, the Seven Holy Archangels and the Most Holy Quimbanda Trinity to manifest here to me and take my command.

THE SACRED CONJURATION OF EXU MARCHOSIAS

I, N.N., a servant of Nzambi, call upon Exu Marchosias, and conjure thee by the power of Exu Maioral and the Divine Sword of Exu, the fire of the Archangel Metatron, the Seven Holy Archangels and the Most Holy Quimbanda Trinity to manifest here to me and take my command.

THE SACRED CONJURATION OF EXU STOLAS

I, N.N., a servant of Nzambi, call upon Exu Stolas, and conjure thee by the power of Exu Maioral and the Divine Sword of Exu, the fire of the Archangel Metatron, the Seven Holy Archangels and the Most Holy Quimbanda Trinity to manifest here to me and take my command.

THE SACRED CONJURATION OF EXU PHENEX

I, N.N., a servant of Nzambi, call upon Exu Phenex, and conjure thee by the power of Exu Maioral and the Divine Sword of Exu, the fire of the Archangel Metatron, the Seven Holy Archangels and the Most Holy Quimbanda Trinity to manifest here to me and take my command.

THE SACRED CONJURATION OF EXU HALPHAS

I, N.N., a servant of Nzambi, call upon Exu Halphas, and conjure thee by the power of Exu Maioral and the Divine Sword of Exu, the fire of the Archangel Metatron, the Seven Holy Archangels and the Most Holy Quimbanda Trinity to manifest here to me and take my command.

THE SACRED CONJURATION OF EXU MALPHAS

I, N.N., a servant of Nzambi, call upon Exu Malphas, and conjure thee by the power of Exu Maioral and the Divine Sword of Exu, the fire of the Archangel Metatron, the Seven Holy Archangels and the Most Holy Quimbanda Trinity to manifest here to me and take my command.

THE SACRED CONJURATION OF EXU RAUM

I, N.N., a servant of Nzambi, call upon Exu Raum, and conjure thee by the power of Exu Maioral and the Divine Sword of Exu, the fire of the Archangel Metatron, the Seven Holy Archangels and the Most Holy Quimbanda Trinity to manifest here to me and take my command.

THE SACRED CONJURATION OF EXU FOCALOR

I, N.N., a servant of Nzambi, call upon Exu Focalor, and conjure thee by the power of Exu Maioral and the Divine Sword of Exu, the fire of the Archangel Metatron, the Seven Holy Archangels and the Most Holy Quimbanda Trinity to manifest here to me and take my command.

THE SACRED CONJURATION OF EXU VEPAR

I, N.N., a servant of Nzambi, call upon Exu Vepar, and conjure thee by the power of Exu Maioral and the Divine Sword of Exu, the fire of the Archangel Metatron, the Seven Holy Archangels and the Most Holy Quimbanda Trinity to manifest here to me and take my command.

THE SACRED CONJURATION OF EXU SABNOCK

I, N.N., a servant of Nzambi, call upon Exu Sabnock, and conjure thee by the power of Exu Maioral and the Divine Sword of Exu, the fire of the Archangel Metatron, the Seven Holy Archangels and the Most Holy Quimbanda Trinity to manifest here to me and take my command.

THE SACRED CONJURATION OF EXU SHAX

I, N.N., a servant of Nzambi, call upon Exu Shax, and conjure thee by the power of Exu Maioral and the Divine Sword of Exu, the fire of the Archangel Metatron, the Seven Holy Archangels and the Most Holy Quimbanda Trinity to manifest here to me and take my command.

THE SACRED CONJURATION OF EXU VINE

I, N.N., a servant of Nzambi, call upon Exu Vine, and conjure thee by the power of Exu Maioral and the Divine Sword of Exu, the fire of the Archangel Metatron, the Seven Holy Archangels and the Most Holy Quimbanda Trinity to manifest here to me and take my command.

THE SACRED CONJURATION OF EXU BIFRONS

I, N.N., a servant of Nzambi, call upon Exu Bifrons, and conjure thee by the power of Exu Maioral and the Divine Sword of Exu, the fire of the Archangel Metatron, the Seven Holy Archangels and the Most Holy Quimbanda Trinity to manifest here to me and take my command.

THE SACRED CONJURATION OF EXU VUAL

I, N.N., a servant of Nzambi, call upon Exu Vual, and conjure thee by the power of Exu Maioral and the Divine Sword of Exu, the fire of the Archangel Metatron, the Seven Holy Archangels and the Most Holy Quimbanda Trinity to manifest here to me and take my command.

THE SACRED CONJURATION OF EXU HAAGENTI

I, N.N., a servant of Nzambi, call upon Exu Haagenti, and conjure thee by the power of Exu Maioral and the Divine Sword of Exu, the fire of the Archangel Metatron, the Seven Holy Archangels and the Most Holy Quimbanda Trinity to manifest here to me and take my command.

THE SACRED CONJURATION OF EXU CROCELL

I, N.N., a servant of Nzambi, call upon Exu Crocell, and conjure thee by the power of Exu Maioral and the Divine Sword of Exu, the fire of the Archangel Metatron, the Seven Holy Archangels and the Most Holy Quimbanda Trinity to manifest here to me and take my command.

THE SACRED CONJURATION OF EXU FURCAS

I, N.N., a servant of Nzambi, call upon Exu Furcas, and conjure thee by the power of Exu Maioral and the Divine Sword of Exu, the fire of the Archangel Metatron, the Seven Holy Archangels and the Most Holy Quimbanda Trinity to manifest here to me and take my command.

THE SACRED CONJURATION OF EXU BALAM

I, N.N., a servant of Nzambi, call upon Exu Balam, and conjure thee by the power of Exu Maioral and the Divine Sword of Exu, the fire of the Archangel Metatron, the Seven Holy Archangels and the Most Holy Quimbanda Trinity to manifest here to me and take my command.

THE SACRED CONJURATION OF EXU ALLOCES

I, N.N., a servant of Nzambi, call upon Exu Alloces, and conjure thee by the power of Exu Maioral and the Divine Sword of Exu, the fire of the Archangel Metatron, the Seven Holy Archangels and the Most Holy Quimbanda Trinity to manifest here to me and take my command.

THE SACRED CONJURATION OF EXU CAMIO

I, N.N., a servant of Nzambi, call upon Exu Camio, and conjure thee by the power of Exu Maioral and the Divine Sword of Exu, the fire of the Archangel Metatron, the Seven Holy Archangels and the Most Holy Quimbanda Trinity to manifest here to me and take my command.

THE SACRED CONJURATION OF EXU MURMUR

I, N.N., a servant of Nzambi, call upon Exu Murmur, and conjure thee by the power of Exu Maioral and the Divine Sword of Exu, the fire of the Archangel Metatron, the Seven Holy Archangels and the Most Holy Quimbanda Trinity to manifest here to me and take my command.

THE SACRED CONJURATION OF EXU ORBAS

I, N.N., a servant of Nzambi, call upon Exu Orbas, and conjure thee by the power of Exu Maioral and the Divine Sword of Exu, the fire of the Archangel Metatron, the Seven Holy Archangels and the Most Holy Quimbanda Trinity to manifest here to me and take my command.

THE SACRED CONJURATION OF EXU GREMORY

I, N.N., a servant of Nzambi, call upon Exu Gremory, and conjure thee by the power of Exu Maioral and the Divine Sword of Exu, the fire of the Archangel Metatron, the Seven Holy Archangels and the Most Holy Quimbanda Trinity to manifest here to me and take my command.

THE SACRED CONJURATION OF EXU OSE

I, N.N., a servant of Nzambi, call upon Exu Ose, and conjure thee by the power of Exu Maioral and the Divine Sword of Exu, the fire of the Archangel Metatron, the Seven Holy Archangels and the Most Holy Quimbanda Trinity to manifest here to me and take my command.

THE SACRED CONJURATION OF EXU AMY

I, N.N., a servant of Nzambi, call upon Exu Amy, and conjure thee by the power of Exu Maioral and the Divine Sword of Exu, the fire of the Archangel Metatron, the Seven Holy Archangels and the Most Holy Quimbanda Trinity to manifest here to me and take my command.

THE SACRED CONJURATION OF EXU ORIAS

I, N.N., a servant of Nzambi, call upon Exu Orias, and conjure thee by the power of Exu Maioral and the Divine Sword of Exu, the fire of the Archangel Metatron, the Seven Holy Archangels and the Most Holy Quimbanda Trinity to manifest here to me and take my command.

THE SACRED CONJURATION OF EXU VAPULA

I, N.N., a servant of Nzambi, call upon Exu Vapula, and conjure thee by the power of Exu Maioral and the Divine Sword of Exu, the fire of the Archangel Metatron, the Seven Holy Archangels and the Most Holy Quimbanda Trinity to manifest here to me and take my command.

THE SACRED CONJURATION OF EXU ZAGAN

I, N.N., a servant of Nzambi, call upon Exu Zagan, and conjure thee by the power of Exu Maioral and the Divine Sword of Exu, the fire of the Archangel Metatron, the Seven Holy Archangels and the Most Holy Quimbanda Trinity to manifest here to me and take my command.

THE SACRED CONJURATION OF EXU VOLAC

I, N.N., a servant of Nzambi, call upon Exu Volac, and conjure thee by the power of Exu Maioral and the Divine Sword of Exu, the fire of the Archangel Metatron, the Seven Holy Archangels and the Most Holy Quimbanda Trinity to manifest here to me and take my command.

THE SACRED CONJURATION OF EXU ANDRAS

I, N.N., a servant of Nzambi, call upon Exu Andras, and conjure thee by the power of Exu Maioral and the Divine Sword of Exu, the fire of the Archangel Metatron, the Seven Holy Archangels and the Most Holy Quimbanda Trinity to manifest here to me and take my command.

THE SACRED CONJURATION OF EXU HAURES

I, N.N., a servant of Nzambi, call upon Exu Haures, and conjure thee by the power of Exu Maioral and the Divine Sword of Exu, the fire of the Archangel Metatron, the Seven Holy Archangels and the Most Holy Quimbanda Trinity to manifest here to me and take my command.

THE SACRED CONJURATION OF ANDREALPHUS

I, N.N., a servant of Nzambi, call upon Exu Andrealphus, and conjure thee by the power of Exu Maioral and the Divine Sword of Exu, the fire of the Archangel Metatron, the Seven Holy Archangels and the Most Holy Quimbanda Trinity to manifest here to me and take my command.

THE SACRED CONJURATION OF EXU CIMEIES

I, N.N., a servant of Nzambi, call upon Exu Cimeies, and conjure thee by the power of Exu Maioral and the Divine Sword of Exu, the fire of the Archangel Metatron, the Seven Holy Archangels and the Most Holy Quimbanda Trinity to manifest here to me and take my command.

THE SACRED CONJURATION OF EXU AMDUSIAS

I, N.N., a servant of Nzambi, call upon Exu Amdusias, and conjure thee by the power of Exu Maioral and the Divine Sword of Exu, the fire of the Archangel Metatron, the Seven Holy Archangels and the Most Holy Quimbanda Trinity to manifest here to me and take my command.

THE SACRED CONJURATION OF EXU BELIAL

I, N.N., a servant of Nzambi, call upon Exu Belial, and conjure thee by the power of Exu Maioral and the Divine Sword of Exu, the fire of the Archangel Metatron, the Seven Holy Archangels and the Most Holy Quimbanda Trinity to manifest here to me and take my command.

THE SACRED CONJURATION OF EXU DECARABIA

I, N.N., a servant of Nzambi, call upon Exu Decarabia, and conjure thee by the power of Exu Maioral and the Divine Sword of Exu, the fire of the Archangel Metatron, the Seven Holy Archangels and the Most Holy Quimbanda Trinity to manifest here to me and take my command.

THE SACRED CONJURATION OF EXU SEERE

I, N.N., a servant of Nzambi, call upon Exu Seere, and conjure thee by the power of Exu Maioral and the Divine Sword of Exu, the fire of the Archangel Metatron, the Seven Holy Archangels and the Most Holy Quimbanda Trinity to manifest here to me and take my command.

THE SACRED CONJURATION OF EXU DANTALION

I, N.N., a servant of Nzambi, call upon Exu Dantalion, and conjure thee by the power of Exu Maioral and the Divine Sword of Exu, the fire of the Archangel Metatron, the Seven Holy Archangels and the Most Holy Quimbanda Trinity to manifest here to me and take my command.

THE SACRED CONJURATION OF EXU ANDROMALIUS

I, N.N., a servant of Nzambi, call upon Exu Andromalius, and conjure thee by the power of Exu Maioral and the Divine Sword of Exu, the fire of the Archangel Metatron, the Seven Holy Archangels and the Most Holy Quimbanda Trinity to manifest here to me and take my command.

O Mighty and powerful seventy-two guardians of Exu Maioral, to you I call and to you I conjure thee by the power of the Divine Sword of Exu, the fire of the Archangel Metatron, and the Most Holy Quimbanda Trinity to manifest here to me and take my command. By the supreme power of the great Guardians of the Seven Quimbanda Kingdoms who govern over the celestial mysteries of the divine universe and govern over the Heavens. I, N.N.., a servant of Nzambi do summon you and command you to come forth and hear my request. I, N.N.., a servant of Nzambi do summon you and command you to come forth and grant my request. By the power of the Divine Sword of Exu ye shall be commanded to come forth and grant my request, SARAVA

CONJURATIONS OF THE SECOND GREATER KINGDOM

Kneel down in front of the altar of the Quimbanda Trinity on your left knee and do and say the following: Ring a brass bell three times using your right hand.

With the *Divine Sword of Exu* in your right hand, make the sign of the Quimbanda Trinity Cross over your body. The Quimbanda Trinity sign of the Cross is made by touching the hand sequentially to the forehead, lower chest or navel area, and right shoulder, then left shoulder and then placing your hands together in a praying position around the handle of the Divine Sword of Exu and then kissing the *Divine Sword of Exu* three times. This is how to say and do this: present the *Divine Sword of Exu* at the forehead, ***IN THE NAME OF NZAMBI***; present the *Divine Sword of Exu* at the naval, ***IN THE NAME OF EXU MAIORAL***; present the *Divine Sword of Exu* across to the right shoulder, ***IN THE NAME OF EXU REI***; present the *Divine Sword of Exu* across to the right left shoulder, ***IN THE NAME OF MARIA PADILLA REINA***; and finally present the *Divine Sword of Exu* to the center of your heart in a praying position, ***SARAVA***; afterwards kiss your hands that are wraped around the handle of the *Divine Sword of Exu* three times.

After blessing yourself with the Divine Sword of Exu recite the following invocation:

Blessed are you, O Lord Nzambi, for you created the Heavens, the Earth and the Seven Quimbanda Kingdoms to protect and to serve all of mankind. Blessed are you, O Lord Nzambi, for you brought down from the Heavens the Divine Sword of Exu to triumph over and to conquer our enemies. May we worship you and give thanks to thee O powerful King of the Heavens and all your divine glory. Sarava

After reciting the sacred invocation, do the following: Stand up facing the altar of the Quimbanda Trinity in the East and hold the Divine Sword of Exu in your right hand and point it towards the altar and towards the Heavens.

THE CONJURATION RITUAL TO SUMMON THE DEITY, EXU REI

Before reciting the following conjuration do the following ritual: Ring a brass bell three times using your right hand. After ringing the bell three times, with the Divine Sword of Exu in your right hand pointed towards the Holy Quimbanda Trinity altar and towards the Heavens and then say the following ritual conjuration:

IN THE NAME OF EXU REI, I INVOKE THY POWER AND DO SUMMON THY MOST HOLY KINGS AND QUEENS OF THE SEVEN KINGDOMS; Exu Rei Das Encruzilhadas and Pomba Gira Reina Das Encruzilhadas, Exu Rei Dos Cruzeiros and Pomba Gira Reina Dos Cruzeiros, Exu Rei Das Matas and Pomba Gira Reina Das Matas, Exu Rei Kalunga and Pomba Gira Reina Kalunga, Exu Rei Das Almas and Pomba Gira Reina Das Almas, Exu Rei Das Liras and Pomba Gira Reina Das Liras and Exu Rei Da Praia and Pomba Gira Reina Das Sete Praias.

IN THE NAME OF EXU REI, I INVOKE THE POWER AND DO SUMMON THE LEGION OF NINE OF THE SEVEN KINGDOMS; Exu Tranca Ruas, Exu Sete Encruzilhadas, Exu Das Almas, Exu Marabo, Exu Tiriri, Exu Veludo, Exu Morcego, Exu Sete Gargalhadas and Exu Mirim. Exu Tranca Tudo, Exu Kirombo, Exu Sete Cruzeiros, Exu Mangueira, Exu Kaminaloa, Exu Sete Cruzes, Exu 7 Portas, Exu Meia Noite and Exu Kalunga. Exu Quebra Galho, Exu Das Sombras, Exu Das Matas, Exu Das Campinas, Exu Da Serra Negra, Exu Sete Pedras, Exu Sete Cobras, Exu Do Cheiro and Exu Arranca Toco. Exu Porteira, Exu Sete Tumbas, Exu Sete Catacumbas, Exu Da Brasa, Exu Caveira, Exu Kalunga, Exu Corcunda, Exu Sete Cova and Exu Capa Preta. Exu Sete Lombas, Exu Pemba, Exu Maraba, Exu Curado, Exu Nove Luzes, Exu 7 Montanhas, Exu Tata Caveira, Exu Gira Mundo and Exu 7 Poeiras. Exu Dos Infernos, Exu Dos Cabares , Exu Sete Liras, Exu Cigano, Exu Ze Pelintra, Exu Pagao, Exu Da Ganga, Exu Male and Exu Chama Dinheiro. Exu Dos Rios, Exu Das Cachoeiras, Exu Da Pedra

Preta, Exu Marinheiro, Exu Do Lodo, Exu Mare, Exu Bahiano, Exu Dos Ventos and Exu Do Coco.

I INVOKE THE MYSTERIES OF EXU REI FROM THE NORTH.

I INVOKE THE MYSTERIES OF EXU REI FROM THE SOUTH.

I INVOKE THE MYSTERIES OF EXU REI FROM THE EAST.

I INVOKE THE MYSTERIES OF EXU REI FROM THE WEST.

I DO SUMMON YOU TO COME FROM WHERE YOU ARE FROM YOUR WORLD TO MY WORLD. PLACE A RING OF PROTECTIVE LIGHT AROUND ME SO THAT MY ENEMIES WILL NOT SEE ME NOR HEAR WHAT IS ABOUT TO BE PETITIONED IN THIS SACRED PRAYER. EXU REI, YOUR ENEMIES ARE MY ENEMIES AND MY ENEMIES ARE YOUR ENEMIES. EXU REI I ASK THAT YOU BRING ME LIGHT, SO THAT YOU WILL LIGHT MY ROADS IN DARKNESS. I ASK YOU THAT ALL OF THE GOOD THINGS IN MY LIFE THAT WERE TAKEN FROM ME UNJUSTLY AND STOLEN FROM ME BY MY ENEMIES THAT YOU BRING ALL OF THE GOOD THINGS BACK TO ME AND TO MY HANDS AT THIS VERY MOMENT FOR HERE WE STAND TOGETHER TO FIGHT A COMMON ENEMY. EXU REI, YOUR ENEMIES ARE MY ENEMIES AND MY ENEMIES ARE YOUR ENEMIES. I ASK YOU HERE AND NOW THAT WHAT EVER MY ENEMIES HAVE DONE TO ME IN THE PAST, ARE PRESENTLY DOING TO ME OR PLAN TO DO TO ME IN THE FUTURE THAT YOU PUNISH THEM 7 X 3 AND BRING THEM TO THEIR KNEES. WHATEVER THEY HAVE DONE OR PLAN TO DO TO ME REVERSE IT BACK TO THEM IN THE NAME OF DIVINE JUSTICE SO THEY WILL RELIQUISH WHATEVER HOLD THEY HAVE OVER ME AND BE ON THEIR WAY. HEAR ME, O GREAT AND MIGHTY EXU REI, FOR YOUR ARE THE KING OF KINGS AND THE GLORY AND THE POWER SHALL BE YOURS FOREVER SARAVA

THE CONJURATIONS OF THE THIRD GREATER KINGDOM

Kneel down in front of the altar of the Quimbanda Trinity on your left knee and do and say the following: Ring a brass bell three times using your right hand.

With the *Divine Sword of Exu* in your right hand, make the sign of the Quimbanda Trinity Cross over your body. The Quimbanda Trinity sign of the Cross is made by touching the hand sequentially to the forehead, lower chest or navel area, and right shoulder, then left shoulder and then placing your hands together in a praying position around the handle of the Divine Sword of Exu and then kissing the *Divine Sword of Exu* three times. This is how to say and do this: present the *Divine Sword of Exu* at the forehead, ***IN THE NAME OF NZAMBI***; present the *Divine Sword of Exu* at the naval, ***IN THE NAME OF EXU MAIORAL***; present the *Divine Sword of Exu* across to the right shoulder, ***IN THE NAME OF EXU REI***; present the *Divine Sword of Exu* across to the right left shoulder, ***IN THE NAME OF MARIA PADILLA REINA***; and finally present the *Divine Sword of Exu* to the center of your heart in a praying position, ***SARAVA***; afterwards kiss your hands that are wraped around the handle of the *Divine Sword of Exu* three times.

After blessing yourself with the Divine Sword of Exu recite the following invocation:

Blessed are you, O Lord Nzambi, for you created the Heavens, the Earth and the Seven Quimbanda Kingdoms to protect and to serve all of mankind. Blessed are you, O Lord Nzambi, for you brought down from the heavens the Divine Sword of Exu to triumph over and to conquer our enemies. May we worship you and give thanks to thee O powerful King of the Heavens and all your divine glory. Sarava

After reciting the sacred invocation, do the following: Stand up facing the altar of the Quimbanda Trinity in the East and

hold the Divine Sword of Exu in your right hand and point it towards the altar and towards the Heavens.

RITUAL TO SUMMON THE DEITY, MARIA PADILLA REINA

Before reciting the following conjuration do the following ritual: Ring a brass bell three times using your right hand. After ringing the bell three times, with the Divine Sword of Exu in your right hand pointed towards the Holy Quimbanda Trinity altar and towards the Heavens and then say the following ritual conjuration:

IN THE NAME OF MARIA PADILLA REINA, I INVOKE THY POWER AND DO SUMMON THY MOST HOLY QUEENS OF THE SEVEN KINGDOMS; Pomba Gira Reina Das Encruzilhadas, Pomba Gira Reina Dos Cruzeiros, Pomba Gira Reina Das Matas, Pomba Gira Reina Kalunga, Pomba Gira Reina Das Almas,Pomba Gira Reina Das Liras and Pomba Gira Reina Das Sete Praias. O DIVINE AND MOST GLORIOUS MARIA PADILLA REINA, EMPRESS OF THE SEVEN, HEAR MY PRAYER. O DIVINE AND MOST GLORIOUS MARIA PADILLA REINA, EMPRESS TO THE SECRETS OF THE PLANETARY MYSTERIES, HEAR MY PRAYER. O DIVINE AND MOST GLORIOUS MARIA PADILLA REINA, QUEEN OF THE CROSSROADS, HEAR MY PRAYER. O DIVINE AND MOST GLORIOUS MARIA PADILLA REINA, QUEEN OF THE PLEASURES OF LIFE, HEAR MY PRAYER. O DIVINE AND MOST GLORIOUS MARIA PADILLA REINA, UNDER THE PROTECTION OF YOUR SACRED SEVEN POINTED STAR, I INVOKE THY HOLY MYSTERIES FROM THE NORTH. O DIVINE AND MOST GLORIOUS MARIA PADILLA REINA, UNDER THE PROTECTION OF YOUR SACRED SEVEN POINTED STAR, I INVOKE THY HOLY MYSTERIES FROM THE SOUTH. O DIVINE AND MOST GLORIOUS MARIA PADILLA REINA, UNDER THE PROTECTION OF YOUR SACRED SEVEN POINTED STAR, I INVOKE THY HOLY MYSTERIES FROM THE EAST. O DIVINE AND MOST GLORIOUS MARIA PADILLA REINA, UNDER THE PROTECTION OF YOUR SACRED SEVEN POINTED STAR, I INVOKE THY HOLY MYSTERIES FROM THE WEST. I DO SUMMON YOU TO COME FROM WHERE YOU ARE FROM YOUR WORLD TO MY WORLD. PLACE A RING OF PROTECTIVE LIGHT AROUND ME SO THAT MY ENEMIES WILL NOT SEE ME NOR

HEAR WHAT IS ABOUT TO BE PETITIONED IN THIS SACRED PRAYER. MARIA PADILLA REINA, YOUR ENEMIES ARE MY ENEMIES AND MY ENEMIES ARE YOUR ENEMIES. MARIA PADILLA REINA I ASK THAT YOU BRING ME LIGHT, SO THAT YOU WILL LIGHT MY ROADS IN DARKNESS. I ASK YOU THAT ALL OF THE GOOD THINGS IN MY LIFE THAT WERE TAKEN FROM ME UNJUSTLY AND STOLEN FROM ME BY MY ENEMIES THAT YOU BRING ALL OF THE GOOD THINGS BACK TO ME AND TO MY HANDS AT THIS VERY MOMENT FOR HERE WE STAND TOGETHER TO FIGHT A COMMON ENEMY. MARIA PADILLA REINA, YOUR ENEMIES ARE MY ENEMIES AND MY ENEMIES ARE YOUR ENEMIES. I ASK YOU HERE AND NOW THAT WHAT EVER MY ENEMIES HAVE DONE TO ME IN THE PAST, ARE PRESENTLY DOING TO ME OR PLAN TO DO TO ME IN THE FUTURE THAT YOU PUNISH THEM 7 X 3 AND BRING THEM TO THEIR KNEES. WHATEVER THEY HAVE DONE OR PLAN TO DO TO ME REVERSE IT BACK TO THEM IN THE NAME OF DIVINE JUSTICE SO THEY WILL RELIQUISH WHATEVER HOLD THEY HAVE OVER ME AND BE ON THEIR WAY. HAIL HOLY QUEEN, DIVINE MOTHER OF GRACE. HEAR ME, O DIVINE AND MOST GLORIOUS MARIA PADILLA REINA, FOR YOUR ARE THE QUEEN OF QUEENS AND THE GLORY AND THE POWER SHALL BE YOURS FOREVER - SARAVA

THE CONJURATIONS OF THE SEVEN LESSER KINGDOMS

Kneel down in front of the altar of the Quimbanda Trinity on your left knee and do and say the following: Ring a brass bell three times using your right hand.

With the *Divine Sword of Exu* in your right hand, make the sign of the Quimbanda Trinity Cross over your body. The Quimbanda Trinity sign of the Cross is made by touching the hand sequentially to the forehead, lower chest or navel area, and right shoulder, then left shoulder and then placing your hands together in a praying position around the handle of the Divine Sword of Exu and then kissing the *Divine Sword of Exu* three times. This is how to say and do this: present the *Divine Sword of Exu* at the forehead, ***IN THE NAME OF NZAMBI***; present the *Divine Sword of Exu* at the naval, ***IN THE NAME OF EXU MAIORAL***; present the *Divine Sword of Exu* across to the right shoulder, ***IN THE NAME OF EXU REI***; present the *Divine Sword of Exu* across to the right left shoulder, ***IN THE NAME OF MARIA PADILLA REINA***; and finally present the *Divine Sword of Exu* to the center of your heart in a praying position, ***SARAVA***; afterwards kiss your hands that are wraped around the handle of the *Divine Sword of Exu* three times.

After blessing yourself with the Divine Sword of Exu recite the following invocation:

Blessed are you, O Lord Nzambi, for you created the Heavens, the Earth and the Seven Quimbanda Kingdoms to protect and to serve all of mankind. Blessed are you, O Lord Nzambi, for you brought down from the heavens the Divine Sword of Exu to triumph over and to conquer our enemies. May we worship you and give thanks to thee O powerful King of the Heavens and all your divine glory. Sarava

After reciting the sacred invocation, do the following: Stand up facing the altar of the Quimbanda Trinity in the East and

hold the Divine Sword of Exu in your right hand and point it towards the altar and towards the Heavens.

CONJURATION OF EXU REI DAS ENCRUZILHADAS & POMBA GIRA REINA DAS ENCRUZILHADAS

Before reciting the following conjuration do the following ritual: Kneel down on your left knee in front of the altar of the Holy Quimbanda Trinity facing East and then ring a brass bell three times using your right hand. After ringing the bell three times, stand up with the Divine Sword of Exu in your right hand pointed towards the Holy Quimbanda Trinity altar and towards the Heavens and then say the following ritual conjuration:

I, N.N., a servant of Nzambi, call upon the Spirit, Exu Rei Das Encruzilhadas and the Spirit, Pomba Gira Reina Das Enchuzilhadas, the Lord and Lady of the Crossroads who govern and command the nine Chief Guardian Spirits of Exu of this realm and do conjure thee by the power of the Divine Sword of Exu and thy Most Holy Quimbanda Trinity to manifest here to me and take my command. By the supreme power of the great Guardians of the Seven Quimbanda Kingdoms who govern over the celestial mysteries of the divine universe and govern over the Heavens. I, N.N.., a servant of Nzambi do summon you and command you to come forth and hear my request. I, N.N.., a servant of Nzambi do summon you and command you to come forth and grant my request. By the power of the Divine Sword of Exu ye shall be commanded to come forth and grant my request, SARAVA

THE SACRED CONJURATION RITUAL OF EXU TRANCA RUAS

I, N.N., a servant of Nzambi, call upon the Chief Guardian Spirit, Exu Tranca Ruas of the Kingdom of the Crossroads and conjure thee by the power of the Divine Sword of Exu through the intercession of the Lord and Lady of the Crossroads, Exu Rei Das Encruzilhadas and Pomba Gira Reina Das Encruzilhadas and thy Most Holy Quimbanda Trinity to manifest here to me and take my command.

THE CONJURATION RITUAL OF EXU SETE ENCRUZILHADAS

I, N.N., a servant of Nzambi, call upon the Chief Guardian Spirit, Exu Sete Encruzilhadas of the Kingdom of the Crossroads and conjure thee by the power of the Divine Sword of Exu through the intercession of the Lord and Lady of the Crossroads, Exu Rei Das Encruzilhadas and Pomba Gira Reina Das Encruzilhadas and thy Most Holy Quimbanda Trinity to manifest here to me and take my command. SARAVA

THE SACRED CONJURATION RITUAL OF EXU DAS ALMAS

I, N.N., a servant of Nzambi, call upon the Chief Guardian Spirit, Exu Das Almas of the Kingdom of the Crossroads and conjure thee by the power of the Divine Sword of Exu through the intercession of the Lord and Lady of the Crossroads, Exu Rei Das Encruzilhadas and Pomba Gira Reina Das Encruzilhadas and thy Most Holy Quimbanda Trinity to manifest here to me and take my command. SARAVA

THE SACRED CONJURATION RITUAL OF EXU MARABO

I, N.N., a servant of Nzambi, call upon the Chief Guardian Spirit, Exu Marabo of the Kingdom of the Crossroads and conjure thee by the power of the Divine Sword of Exu through the intercession of the Lord and Lady of the Crossroads, Exu Rei Das Encruzilhadas and Pomba Gira Reina Das Encruzilhadas and thy Most Holy Quimbanda Trinity to manifest here to me and take my command. SARAVA

THE SACRED CONJURATION RITUAL OF EXU TIRIRI

I, N.N., a servant of Nzambi, call upon the Chief Guardian Spirit, Exu Tiriri of the Kingdom of the Crossroads and conjure thee by the power of the Divine Sword of Exu through the intercession of the Lord and Lady of the Crossroads, Exu Rei Das Encruzilhadas and Pomba Gira Reina Das Encruzilhadas and thy Most Holy Quimbanda Trinity to manifest here to me and take my command. SARAVA

THE SACRED CONJURATION RITUAL OF EXU VELUDO

I, N.N., a servant of Nzambi, call upon the Chief Guardian Spirit, Exu Veludo of the Kingdom of the Crossroads and conjure thee by the power of the Divine Sword of Exu through the intercession of the Lord and Lady of the Crossroads, Exu Rei Das Encruzilhadas and Pomba Gira Reina Das Encruzilhadas and thy Most Holy Quimbanda Trinity to manifest here to me and take my command. SARAVA

THE SACRED CONJURATION RITUAL OF EXU MORCEGO

I, N.N., a servant of Nzambi, call upon the Chief Guardian Spirit, Exu Morcego of the Kingdom of the Crossroads and conjure thee by the power of the Divine Sword of Exu through the intercession of the Lord and Lady of the Crossroads, Exu Rei Das Encruzilhadas and Pomba Gira Reina Das Encruzilhadas and thy Most Holy Quimbanda Trinity to manifest here to me and take my command. SARAVA

THE CONJURATION RITUAL OF EXU SETE GARGALHADAS

I, N.N., a servant of Nzambi, call upon the Chief Guardian Spirit, Exu Gargalhadas of the Kingdom of the Crossroads and conjure thee by the power of the Divine Sword of Exu through the intercession of the Lord and Lady of the Crossroads, Exu Rei Das Encruzilhadas and Pomba Gira Reina Das Encruzilhadas and thy Most Holy Quimbanda Trinity to manifest here to me and take my command. SARAVA

THE SACRED CONJURATION RITUAL OF EXU MIRIM

I, N.N., a servant of Nzambi, call upon the Chief Guardian Spirit, Exu Mirim of the Kingdom of the Crossroads and conjure thee by the power of the Divine Sword of Exu through the intercession of the Lord and Lady of the Crossroads, Exu Rei Das Encruzilhadas and Pomba Gira Reina Das Encruzilhadas and thy Most Holy Quimbanda

Trinity to manifest here to me and take my command. SARAVA

CONJURATION OF EXU REI DOS CRUZEIROS & POMBA GIRA REINA DOS CRUZEIROS

I, N.N., a servant of Nzambi, call upon the Spirit, Exu Rei Dos Cruzeiros and the Spirit, Pomba Gira Reina Dos Cruzeiros, the Lord and Lady of the Crossings who govern and command the nine Chief Guardian Spirits of Exu of this realm and do conjure thee by the power of the Divine Sword of Exu and thy Most Holy Quimbanda Trinity to manifest here to me and take my command. SARAVA

THE SACRED CONJURATION RITUAL OF EXU TRANCA TUDO

I, N.N., a servant of Nzambi, call upon the Chief Guardian Spirit, Exu Tranca Tudo of the Kingdom of the Crossings and conjure thee by the power of the Divine Sword of Exu through the intercession of the Lord and Lady of the Crossings, Exu Rei Dos Cruzeiros and Pomba Gira Reina Dos Cruzeiros and thy Most Holy Quimbanda Trinity to manifest here to me and take my command. SARAVA

THE SACRED CONJURATION RITUAL OF EXU KIROMBO

I, N.N., a servant of Nzambi, call upon the Chief Guardian Spirit, Exu Kirombo of the Kingdom of the Crossings and conjure thee by the power of the Divine Sword of Exu through the intercession of the Lord and Lady of the Crossings, Exu Rei Dos Cruzeiros and Pomba Gira Reina Dos Cruzeiros and thy Most Holy Quimbanda Trinity to manifest here to me and take my command. SARAVA

THE SACRED CONJURATION RITUAL OF EXU SETE CRUZEIROS

I, N.N., a servant of Nzambi, call upon the Chief Guardian Spirit, Exu Sete Cruzeiros of the Kingdom of the Crossings and conjure thee by the power of the Divine Sword of Exu through the intercession of the Lord and Lady of the Crossings, Exu Rei Dos Cruzeiros and Pomba Gira Reina Dos Cruzeiros and thy Most Holy Quimbanda Trinity to manifest here to me and take my command.

THE SACRED CONJURATION RITUAL OF EXU MANGUEIRA

I, N.N., a servant of Nzambi, call upon the Chief Guardian Spirit, Exu Mangueira of the Kingdom of the Crossings and conjure thee by the power of the Divine Sword of Exu through the intercession of the Lord and Lady of the Crossings, Exu Rei Dos Cruzeiros and Pomba Gira Reina Dos Cruzeiros and thy Most Holy Quimbanda Trinity to manifest here to me and take my command. SARAVA

THE SACRED CONJURATION RITUAL OF EXU KAMINALOA

I, N.N., a servant of Nzambi, call upon the Chief Guardian Spirit, Exu Kiminaloa of the Kingdom of the Crossings and conjure thee by the power of the Divine Sword of Exu through the intercession of the Lord and Lady of the Crossings, Exu Rei Dos Cruzeiros and Pomba Gira Reina Dos Cruzeiros and thy Most Holy Quimbanda Trinity to manifest here to me and take my command. SARAVA

THE SACRED CONJURATION RITUAL OF EXU SETE CRUZES

I, N.N., a servant of Nzambi, call upon the Chief Guardian Spirit, Exu Sete Cruzes of the Kingdom of the Crossings and conjure thee by the power of the Divine Sword of Exu through the intercession of the Lord and Lady of the Crossings, Exu Rei Dos Cruzeiros and Pomba Gira Reina Dos Cruzeiros and thy Most Holy Quimbanda Trinity to manifest here to me and take my command. SARAVA

THE SACRED CONJURATION RITUAL OF EXU SETE PORTAS

I, N.N., a servant of Nzambi, call upon the Chief Guardian Spirit, Exu Sete Portas of the Kingdom of the Crossings and conjure thee by the power of the Divine Sword of Exu through the intercession of the Lord and Lady of the Crossings, Exu Rei Dos Cruzeiros and Pomba Gira Reina Dos Cruzeiros and thy Most Holy Quimbanda Trinity to manifest here to me and take my command. SARAVA

THE SACRED CONJURATION RITUAL OF EXU MEIA NOITE

I, N.N., a servant of Nzambi, call upon the Chief Guardian Spirit, Exu Meia Noite of the Kingdom of the Crossings and conjure thee by the power of the Divine Sword of Exu through the intercession of the Lord and Lady of the Crossings, Exu Rei Dos Cruzeiros and Pomba Gira Reina Dos Cruzeiros and thy Most Holy Quimbanda Trinity to manifest here to me and take my command. SARAVA

THE SACRED CONJURATION RITUAL OF EXU KALUNGA

I, N.N., a servant of Nzambi, call upon the Chief Guardian Spirit, Exu Kalunga of the Kingdom of the Crossings and conjure thee by the power of the Divine Sword of Exu through the intercession of the Lord and Lady of the Crossings, Exu Rei Dos Cruzeiros and Pomba Gira Reina Dos Cruzeiros and thy Most Holy Quimbanda Trinity to manifest here to me and take my command. SARAVA

CONJURATION OF EXU REI DAS MATAS & POMBA GIRA REINA DAS MATAS

I, N.N., a servant of Nzambi, call upon the Spirit, Exu Rei Das Matas and the Spirit, Pomba Gira Reina Das Matas, the Lord and Lady of the Forest who govern and command the nine Chief Guardian Spirits of Exu of this realm and do conjure thee by the power of the Divine Sword of Exu and thy Most Holy Quimbanda Trinity to manifest here to me and take my command.

THE SACRED CONJURATION RITUAL OF EXU QUEBRA GALHO

I, N.N., a servant of Nzambi, call upon the Chief Guardian Spirit, Exu Quebra Galho of the Kingdom of the Forest and conjure thee by the power of the Divine Sword of Exu through the intercession of the Lord and Lady of the Forest, Exu Rei Das Matas and Pomba Gira Reina Das Matas and thy Most Holy Quimbanda Trinity to manifest here to me and take my command. SARAVA

THE SACRED CONJURATION RITUAL OF EXU DAS SOMBRAS

I, N.N., a servant of Nzambi, call upon the Chief Guardian Spirit, Exu Das Sombras of the Kingdom of the Forest and conjure thee by the power of the Divine Sword of Exu through the intercession of the Lord and Lady of the Forest, Exu Rei Das Matas and Pomba Gira Reina Das Matas and thy Most Holy Quimbanda Trinity to manifest here to me and take my command. SARAVA

THE SACRED CONJURATION RITUAL OF EXU DAS MATAS

I, N.N., a servant of Nzambi, call upon the Chief Guardian Spirit, Exu Das Matas of the Kingdom of the Forest and conjure thee by the power of the Divine Sword of Exu through the intercession of the Lord and Lady of the Forest, Exu Rei Das Matas and Pomba Gira Reina Das Matas and thy Most Holy Quimbanda Trinity to manifest here to me and take my command. SARAVA

THE SACRED CONJURATION RITUAL OF EXU DAS CAMPINAS

I, N.N., a servant of Nzambi, call upon the Chief Guardian Spirit, Exu Das Campinas of the Kingdom of the Forest and conjure thee by the power of the Divine Sword of Exu through the intercession of the Lord and Lady of the Forest, Exu Rei Das Matas and Pomba Gira Reina Das Matas and thy Most Holy Quimbanda Trinity to manifest here to me and take my command. SARAVA

THE SACRED CONJURATION RITUAL OF EXU DA SERRA NEGRA

I, N.N., a servant of Nzambi, call upon the Chief Guardian Spirit, Exu Da Serra Negra of the Kingdom of the Forest and conjure thee by the power of the Divine Sword of Exu through the intercession of the Lord and Lady of the Forest, Exu Rei Das Matas and Pomba Gira Reina Das Matas and thy Most Holy Quimbanda Trinity to manifest here to me and take my command. SARAVA

THE SACRED CONJURATION RITUAL OF EXU SETE PEDRAS

I, N.N., a servant of Nzambi, call upon the Chief Guardian Spirit, Exu Sete Pedras of the Kingdom of the Forest and conjure thee by the power of the Divine Sword of Exu through the intercession of the Lord and Lady of the Forest, Exu Rei Das Matas and Pomba Gira Reina Das Matas and thy Most Holy Quimbanda Trinity to manifest here to me and take my command. SARAVA

THE SACRED CONJURATION RITUAL OF EXU SETE COBRAS

I, N.N., a servant of Nzambi, call upon the Chief Guardian Spirit, Exu Sete Cobras of the Kingdom of the Forest and conjure thee by the power of the Divine Sword of Exu through the intercession of the Lord and Lady of the Forest, Exu Rei Das Matas and Pomba Gira Reina Das Matas and thy Most Holy Quimbanda Trinity to manifest here to me and take my command. Sarava

THE SACRED CONJURATION RITUAL OF EXU DO CHEIRO

I, N.N., a servant of Nzambi, call upon the Chief Guardian Spirit, Exu Do Cheiro of the Kingdom of the Forest and conjure thee by the power of the Divine Sword of Exu through the intercession of the Lord and Lady of the Forest, Exu Rei Das Matas and Pomba Gira Reina Das Matas and thy Most Holy Quimbanda Trinity to manifest here to me and take my command. SARAVA

THE SACRED CONJURATION RITUAL OF EXU ARRANCA TOCO

I, N.N., a servant of Nzambi, call upon the Chief Guardian Spirit, Exu Arranca Toco of the Kingdom of the Forest and conjure thee by the power of the Divine Sword of Exu through the intercession of the Lord and Lady of the Forest, Exu Rei Das Matas and Pomba Gira Reina Das Matas and thy Most Holy Quimbanda Trinity to manifest here to me and take my command. SARAVA

CONJURATION OF EXU REI KALUNGA & POMBA GIRA REINA DA KALUNGA

I, N.N., a servant of Nzambi, call upon the Spirit, Exu Rei Da Kalunga and the Spirit, Pomba Gira Reina Da Kalunga, the Lord and Lady of the Cemetery who govern and command the nine Chief Guardian Spirits of Exu of this realm and do conjure thee by the power of the Divine Sword of Exu and thy Most Holy Quimbanda Trinity to manifest here to me and take my command. SARAVA

THE SACRED CONJURATION RITUAL OF EXU PORTEIRA

I, N.N., a servant of Nzambi, call upon the Chief Guardian Spirit, Exu Porteira of the Kingdom of the Cemetery and conjure thee by the power of the Divine Sword of Exu through the intercession of the Lord and Lady of the Cemetery, Exu Rei Da Kalunga and Pomba Gira Reina Da Kalunga and thy Most Holy Quimbanda Trinity to manifest here to me and take my command. SARAVA

THE SACRED CONJURATION RITUAL OF EXU SETE TUMBAS

I, N.N., a servant of Nzambi, call upon the Chief Guardian Spirit, Exu Sete Tumbas of the Kingdom of the Cemetery and conjure thee by the power of the Divine Sword of Exu through the intercession of the Lord and Lady of the Cemetery, Exu Rei Da Kalunga and Pomba Gira Reina Da Kalunga and thy Most Holy Quimbanda Trinity to manifest here to me and take my command. SARAVA

THE CONJURATION RITUAL OF EXU SETE CATACUMBAS

I, N.N., a servant of Nzambi, call upon the Chief Guardian Spirit, Exu Sete Ctatcumbas of the Kingdom of the Cemetery and conjure thee by the power of the Divine Sword of Exu through the intercession of the Lord and Lady of the Cemetery, Exu Rei Da Kalunga and Pomba Gira Reina Da Kalunga and thy Most Holy Quimbanda Trinity to manifest here to me and take my command. SARAVA

THE SACRED CONJURATION RITUAL OF EXU DA BRASA

I, N.N., a servant of Nzambi, call upon the Chief Guardian Spirit, Exu Da Brasa of the Kingdom of the Cemetery and conjure thee by the power of the Divine Sword of Exu through the intercession of the Lord and Lady of the Cemetery, Exu Rei Da Kalunga and Pomba Gira Reina Da Kalunga and thy Most Holy Quimbanda Trinity to manifest here to me and take my command. SARAVA

THE SACRED CONJURATION RITUAL OF EXU CAVEIRA

I, N.N., a servant of Nzambi, call upon the Chief Guardian Spirit, Exu Caveira of the Kingdom of the Cemetery and conjure thee by the power of the Divine Sword of Exu through the intercession of the Lord and Lady of the Cemetery, Exu Rei Da Kalunga and Pomba Gira Reina Da Kalunga and thy Most Holy Quimbanda Trinity to manifest here to me and take my command. SARAVA

THE CONJURATION RITUAL OF EXU KALUNGA PEQUENA

I, N.N., a servant of Nzambi, call upon the Chief Guardian Spirit, Exu Kalunga Pequena of the Kingdom of the Cemetery and conjure thee by the power of the Divine Sword of Exu through the intercession of the Lord and Lady of the Cemetery, Exu Rei Da Kalunga and Pomba Gira Reina Da Kalunga and thy Most Holy Quimbanda Trinity to manifest here to me and take my command. SARAVA

THE SACRED CONJURATION RITUAL OF EXU CORCUNDA

I, N.N., a servant of Nzambi, call upon the Chief Guardian Spirit, Exu Corcunda of the Kingdom of the Cemetery and conjure thee by the power of the Divine Sword of Exu through the intercession of the Lord and Lady of the Cemetery, Exu Rei Da Kalunga and Pomba Gira Reina Da Kalunga and thy Most Holy Quimbanda Trinity to manifest here to me and take my command. SARAVA

THE SACRED CONJURATION RITUAL OF EXU SETE COVAS

I, N.N., a servant of Nzambi, call upon the Chief Guardian Spirit, Exu Sete Covas of the Kingdom of the Cemetery and conjure thee by the power of the Divine Sword of Exu through the intercession of the Lord and Lady of the Cemetery, Exu Rei Da Kalunga and Pomba Gira Reina Da Kalunga and thy Most Holy Quimbanda Trinity to manifest here to me and take my command. SARAVA

THE SACRED CONJURATION RITUAL OF EXU CAPA PRETA

I, N.N., a servant of Nzambi, call upon the Chief Guardian Spirit, Exu Capa Preta of the Kingdom of the Cemetery and conjure thee by the power of the Divine Sword of Exu through the intercession of the Lord and Lady of the Cemetery, Exu Rei Da Kalunga and Pomba Gira Reina Da Kalunga and thy Most Holy Quimbanda Trinity to manifest here to me and take my command. SARAVA

CONJURATION OF EXU REI DAS ALMAS & POMBA GIRA REINA DAS ALMAS

I, N.N., a servant of Nzambi, call upon the Spirit, Exu Rei Das Almas and the Spirit, Pomba Gira Reina Das Almas, the Lord and Lady of the Souls who govern and command the nine Chief Guardian Spirits of Exu of this realm and do conjure thee by the power of the Divine Sword of Exu and thy Most Holy Quimbanda Trinity to manifest here to me and take my command. SARAVA

THE SACRED CONJURATION RITUAL OF EXU SETE LOMBAS

I, N.N., a servant of Nzambi, call upon the Chief Guardian Spirit, Exu Sete Lombas of the Kingdom of the Souls and conjure thee by the power of the Divine Sword of Exu through the intercession of the Lord and Lady of the Kingdom of Souls, Exu Rei Das Almas and Pomba Gira Reina Das Almas and thy Most Holy Quimbanda Trinity to manifest here to me and take my command. SARAVA

THE SACRED CONJURATION RITUAL OF EXU PEMBA

I, N.N., a servant of Nzambi, call upon the Chief Guardian Spirit, Exu Pemba of the Kingdom of the Souls and conjure thee by the power of the Divine Sword of Exu through the intercession of the Lord and Lady of the Kingdom of Souls, Exu Rei Das Almas and Pomba Gira Reina Das Almas and thy Most Holy Quimbanda Trinity to manifest here to me and take my command. SARAVA

THE SACRED CONJURATION RITUAL OF EXU MARABA

I, N.N., a servant of Nzambi, call upon the Chief Guardian Spirit, Exu Maraba of the Kingdom of the Souls and conjure thee by the power of the Divine Sword of Exu through the intercession of the Lord and Lady of the Kingdom of Souls, Exu Rei Das Almas and Pomba Gira Reina Das Almas and thy Most Holy Quimbanda Trinity to manifest here to me and take my command. SARAVA

THE SACRED CONJURATION RITUAL OF EXU CURADO

I, N.N., a servant of Nzambi, call upon the Chief Guardian Spirit, Exu Curado of the Kingdom of the Souls and conjure thee by the power of the Divine Sword of Exu through the intercession of the Lord and Lady of the Kingdom of Souls, Exu Rei Das Almas and Pomba Gira Reina Das Almas and thy Most Holy Quimbanda Trinity to manifest here to me and take my command. SARAVA

THE SACRED CONJURATION RITUAL OF EXU NOVE LUZES

I, N.N., a servant of Nzambi, call upon the Chief Guardian Spirit, Exu Nove Luzes of the Kingdom of the Souls and conjure thee by the power of the Divine Sword of Exu through the intercession of the Lord and Lady of the Kingdom of Souls, Exu Rei Das Almas and Pomba Gira Reina Das Almas and thy Most Holy Quimbanda Trinity to manifest here to me and take my command. SARAVA

THE SACRED CONJURATION RITUAL OF EXU SETE MONTANHAS

I, N.N., a servant of Nzambi, call upon the Chief Guardian Spirit, Exu Sete Montanhas of the Kingdom of the Souls and conjure thee by the power of the Divine Sword of Exu through the intercession of the Lord and Lady of the Kingdom of Souls, Exu Rei Das Almas and Pomba Gira Reina Das Almas and thy Most Holy Quimbanda Trinity to manifest here to me and take my command. SARAVA

THE SACRED CONJURATION RITUAL OF EXU TATA CAVEIRA

I, N.N., a servant of Nzambi, call upon the Chief Guardian Spirit, Exu Tata Caveira of the Kingdom of the Souls and conjure thee by the power of the Divine Sword of Exu through the intercession of the Lord and Lady of the Kingdom of Souls, Exu Rei Das Almas and Pomba Gira Reina Das Almas and thy Most Holy Quimbanda Trinity to manifest here to me and take my command. SARAVA

THE SACRED CONJURATION RITUAL OF EXU GIRA MUNDO

I, N.N., a servant of Nzambi, call upon the Chief Guardian Spirit, Exu Gira Mundo of the Kingdom of the Souls and conjure thee by the power of the Divine Sword of Exu through the intercession of the Lord and Lady of the Kingdom of Souls, Exu Rei Das Almas and Pomba Gira Reina Das Almas and thy Most Holy Quimbanda Trinity to manifest here to me and take my command. SARAVA

THE SACRED CONJURATION RITUAL OF EXU SETE POEIRAS

I, N.N., a servant of Nzambi, call upon the Chief Guardian Spirit, Exu Sete Poeiras of the Kingdom of the Souls and conjure thee by the power of the Divine Sword of Exu through the intercession of the Lord and Lady of the Kingdom of Souls, Exu Rei Das Almas and Pomba Gira Reina Das Almas and thy Most Holy Quimbanda Trinity to manifest here to me and take my command. SARAVA

CONJURATION OF EXU REI DAS LIRAS & POMBA GIRA REINA DAS LIRAS

I, N.N., a servant of Nzambi, call upon the Spirit, Exu Rei Das Liras and the Spirit, Pomba Gira Reina Das Liras, the Lord and Lady of the Kingdom of Lyre who govern and command the nine Chief Guardian Spirits of Exu of this realm and do conjure thee by the power of the Divine Sword of Exu and thy Most Holy Quimbanda Trinity to manifest here to me and take my command. SARAVA

THE SACRED CONJURATION RITUAL OF EXU DOS INFERNOS

I, N.N., a servant of Nzambi, call upon the Chief Guardian Spirit, Exu Dos Infernos of the Kingdom of the Lyre and conjure thee by the power of the Divine Sword of Exu through the intercession of the Lord and Lady of the Kingdom of Lyre, Exu Rei Das Liras and Pomba Gira Reina Das Liras and thy Most Holy Quimbanda Trinity to manifest here to me and take my command. SARAVA

THE SACRED CONJURATION RITUAL OF EXU DOS CABARES

I, N.N., a servant of Nzambi, call upon the Chief Guardian Spirit, Exu Dos Cabares of the Kingdom of the Lyre and conjure thee by the power of the Divine Sword of Exu through the intercession of the Lord and Lady of the Kingdom of Lyre, Exu Rei Das Liras and Pomba Gira Reina Das Liras and thy Most Holy Quimbanda Trinity to manifest here to me and take my command. SARAVA

THE SACRED CONJURATION RITUAL OF EXU SETE LIRAS

I, N.N., a servant of Nzambi, call upon the Chief Guardian Spirit, Exu Sete Liras of the Kingdom of the Lyre and conjure thee by the power of the Divine Sword of Exu through the intercession of the Lord and Lady of the Kingdom of Lyre, Exu Rei Das Liras and Pomba Gira Reina Das Liras and thy Most Holy Quimbanda Trinity to manifest here to me and take my command. SARAVA

THE SACRED CONJURATION RITUAL OF EXU CIGANO

I, N.N., a servant of Nzambi, call upon the Chief Guardian Spirit, Exu Cigano of the Kingdom of the Lyre and conjure thee by the power of the Divine Sword of Exu through the intercession of the Lord and Lady of the Kingdom of Lyre, Exu Rei Das Liras and Pomba Gira Reina Das Liras and thy Most Holy Quimbanda Trinity to manifest here to me and take my command. SARAVA

THE SACRED CONJURATION RITUAL OF EXU ZE PELINTRA

I, N.N., a servant of Nzambi, call upon the Chief Guardian Spirit, Exu Ze Pelintra of the Kingdom of the Lyre and conjure thee by the power of the Divine Sword of Exu through the intercession of the Lord and Lady of the Kingdom of Lyre, Exu Rei Das Liras and Pomba Gira Reina Das Liras and thy Most Holy Quimbanda Trinity to manifest here to me and take my command. SARAVA

THE SACRED CONJURATION RITUAL OF EXU PAGAO

I, N.N., a servant of Nzambi, call upon the Chief Guardian Spirit, Exu Pagao of the Kingdom of the Lyre and conjure thee by the power of the Divine Sword of Exu through the intercession of the Lord and Lady of the Kingdom of Lyre, Exu Rei Das Liras and Pomba Gira Reina Das Liras and thy Most Holy Quimbanda Trinity to manifest here to me and take my command. SARAVA

THE SACRED CONJURATION RITUAL OF EXU DA GANGA

I, N.N., a servant of Nzambi, call upon the Chief Guardian Spirit, Exu Da Ganga of the Kingdom of the Lyre and conjure thee by the power of the Divine Sword of Exu through the intercession of the Lord and Lady of the Kingdom of Lyre, Exu Rei Das Liras and Pomba Gira Reina Das Liras and thy Most Holy Quimbanda Trinity to manifest here to me and take my command. SARAVA

THE SACRED CONJURATION RITUAL OF EXU MALE

I, N.N., a servant of Nzambi, call upon the Chief Guardian Spirit, Exu Male of the Kingdom of the Lyre and conjure thee by the power of the Divine Sword of Exu through the intercession of the Lord and Lady of the Kingdom of Lyre, Exu Rei Das Liras and Pomba Gira Reina Das Liras and thy Most Holy Quimbanda Trinity to manifest here to me and take my command. SARAVA

THE SACRED CONJURATION RITUAL OF EXU CHAMA DINHEIRO

I, N.N., a servant of Nzambi, call upon the Chief Guardian Spirit, Exu Chama Dinheiro of the Kingdom of the Lyre and conjure thee by the power of the Divine Sword of Exu through the intercession of the Lord and Lady of the Kingdom of Lyre, Exu Rei Das Liras and Pomba Gira Reina Das Liras and thy Most Holy Quimbanda Trinity to manifest here to me and take my command. SARAVA

CONJURATION OF EXU REI DAS SETE PRAIAS & POMBA GIRA REINA DAS SETE PRAIAS

I, N.N., a servant of Nzambi, call upon the Spirit, Exu Rei Das Sete Praias and the Spirit, Pomba Gira Reina Das Sete Praias, the Lord and Lady of the Kingdom of Beaches who govern and command the nine Chief Guardian Spirits of Exu of this realm and do conjure thee by the power of the Divine Sword of Exu and thy Most Holy Quimbanda Trinity to manifest here to me and take my command. SARAVA

THE SACRED CONJURATION RITUAL OF EXU DOS RIOS

I, N.N., a servant of Nzambi, call upon the Chief Guardian Spirit, Exu Dos Rios of the Kingdom of the Beaches and conjure thee by the power of the Divine Sword of Exu through the intercession of the Lord and Lady of the Beaches, Exu Rei Das Sete Praias and Pomba Gira Reina Das Sete Praias and thy Most Holy Quimbanda Trinity to manifest here to me and take my command. SARAVA

THE SACRED CONJURATION RITUAL OF EXU CACHOEIRAS

I, N.N., a servant of Nzambi, call upon the Chief Guardian Spirit, Exu Cachoeiras of the Kingdom of the Beaches and conjure thee by the power of the Divine Sword of Exu through the intercession of the Lord and Lady of the Beaches, Exu Rei Das Sete Praias and Pomba Gira Reina Das Sete Praias and thy Most Holy Quimbanda Trinity to manifest here to me and take my command. SARAVA

THE SACRED CONJURATION RITUAL OF EXU DA PEDRA PRETA

I, N.N., a servant of Nzambi, call upon the Chief Guardian Spirit, Exu Da Pedra Preta of the Kingdom of the Beaches and conjure thee by the power of the Divine Sword of Exu through the intercession of the Lord and Lady of the Beaches, Exu Rei Das Sete Praias and Pomba Gira Reina Das Sete Praias and thy Most Holy Quimbanda Trinity to manifest here to me and take my command. SARAVA

THE SACRED CONJURATION RITUAL OF EXU MARINHEIRO

I, N.N., a servant of Nzambi, call upon the Chief Guardian Spirit, Exu Marinheiro of the Kingdom of the Beaches and conjure thee by the power of the Divine Sword of Exu through the intercession of the Lord and Lady of the Beaches, Exu Rei Das Sete Praias and Pomba Gira Reina Das Sete Praias and thy Most Holy Quimbanda Trinity to manifest here to me and take my command. SARAVA

THE SACRED CONJURATION RITUAL OF EXU DO LODO

I, N.N., a servant of Nzambi, call upon the Chief Guardian Spirit, Exu Do Lodo of the Kingdom of the Beaches and conjure thee by the power of the Divine Sword of Exu through the intercession of the Lord and Lady of the Beaches, Exu Rei Das Sete Praias and Pomba Gira Reina Das Sete Praias and thy Most Holy Quimbanda Trinity to manifest here to me and take my command. SARAVA

THE SACRED CONJURATION RITUAL OF EXU MARE

I, N.N., a servant of Nzambi, call upon the Chief Guardian Spirit, Exu Mare of the Kingdom of the Beaches and conjure thee by the power of the Divine Sword of Exu through the intercession of the Lord and Lady of the Beaches, Exu Rei Das Sete Praias and Pomba Gira Reina Das Sete Praias and thy Most Holy Quimbanda Trinity to manifest here to me and take my command. SARAVA

THE SACRED CONJURATION RITUAL OF EXU BAHIANO

I, N.N., a servant of Nzambi, call upon the Chief Guardian Spirit, Exu Bahiano of the Kingdom of the Beaches and conjure thee by the power of the Divine Sword of Exu through the intercession of the Lord and Lady of the Beaches, Exu Rei Das Sete Praias and Pomba Gira Reina Das Sete Praias and thy Most Holy Quimbanda Trinity to manifest here to me and take my command. SARAVA

THE SACRED CONJURATION RITUAL OF EXU DOS VENTOS

I, N.N., a servant of Nzambi, call upon the Chief Guardian Spirit, Exu Dos Ventos of the Kingdom of the Beaches and conjure thee by the power of the Divine Sword of Exu through the intercession of the Lord and Lady of the Beaches, Exu Rei Das Sete Praias and Pomba Gira Reina Das Sete Praias and thy Most Holy Quimbanda Trinity to manifest here to me and take my command. SARAVA

THE SACRED CONJURATION RITUAL OF EXU DO COCO

I, N.N., a servant of Nzambi, call upon the Chief Guardian Spirit, Exu Do Coco of the Kingdom of the Beaches and conjure thee by the power of the Divine Sword of Exu through the intercession of the Lord and Lady of the Beaches, Exu Rei Das Sete Praias and Pomba Gira Reina Das Sete Praias and thy Most Holy Quimbanda Trinity to manifest here to me and take my command.

By the supreme power of the great Guardians of the Seven Quimbanda Kingdoms who govern over the celestial mysteries of the divine universe and govern over the Heavens. I, N.N.., a servant of Nzambi do summon you and command you to come forth and hear my request. I, N.N.., a servant of Nzambi do summon you and command you to come forth and grant my request. By the power of the Divine Sword of Exu ye shall be commanded to come forth and grant my request, SARAVA.

THE CLOSING CONJURATION RITUAL PRAYER

Kneel down in front of the Quimbanda altar facing the east with the Divine Sword of Exu in both hands and say the following prayer:

O Mighty God, Nzambi who has created all things in the Heavens and the Earth and has given unto me the wisdom of discernment to understand the good and the evil; through thy holy name, Nzambi Mpungo, Nzambi Ntoto and through your Divine power, I do invoke the sacred and holy spirits of the Quimbanda Trinity who are kneeling at the foot of thy throne and who guard and watch over thy Seven Quimbanda Kingdoms of thy realm here on Earth. O Lord, through the Sacred and Holy Divine Sword of Exu in my hands may you grant me that this ritual of Divine justice become true and veritable in my hands. O Nzambi, whose reign and empire remaineth eternally and unto the ages of the ages. In the name of the mighty and holy God! Blessed art thou Nzambi, O Lord our God, King of the Universe, who through this sacred ritual gives me the power to triumph over my enemies. Blessed art thou Nzambi, O Lord our God, King of the Universe, who through this sacred ritual gives me the power to triumph over my enemies. Blessed art thou Nzambi, O Lord our God, King of the Universe, who through this sacred ritual gives me the power to destroy my enemies. Blessed art thou Nzambi, O Lord our God, King of the Universe, who through this sacred ritual gives me the power to conquer over my enemies. O Lord God, Nzambi, who art seated upon the Heavens, and who reigns over the abysses beneath, grant unto me thy grace I beseech thee, so that what I conceive in my mind I may accomplish in my work, through thee, O God, Nzambi, the sovereign ruler of all, who livest and reignest unto the ages of the ages Amen. Exu, may the thunder in my heart become one in the same with the Divine Sword of Exu and strick down my enemies in thy most sacred and divine holy name. Nzambi, by the Divine Sword of Exu I command this ritual into being. Exu by the

Divine Sword of the King of Kings, I lay down my enemies at your feet. Exu by the Divine Sword of the King of Kings, I do bind my enemies in thy most sacred name. Exu by the Divine Sword of the King of Kings, I do blind my enemies in thy most sacred name Exu by the Divine Sword of the King of Kings, I do destroy my enemies in thy most sacred name. Exu by the Divine Sword of the King of Kings, Give me victory to triumph over my enemies. Exu by the Divine Sword of the King of Kings, Give me victory to defeat my enemies. Exu by the Divine Sword of the King of Kings, I wash my hands clean like Pontius Pilate - SARAVA

With the *Divine Sword of Exu* in your right hand, make the sign of the Quimbanda Trinity Cross over your body. The Quimbanda Trinity sign of the Cross is made by touching the hand sequentially to the forehead, lower chest or navel area, and right shoulder, then left shoulder and then placing your hands together in a praying position around the handle of the Divine Sword of Exu and then kissing the *Divine Sword of Exu* three times. This is how to say and do this: present the *Divine Sword of Exu* at the forehead, ***IN THE NAME OF NZAMBI***; present the *Divine Sword of Exu* at the naval, ***IN THE NAME OF EXU MAIORAL***; present the *Divine Sword of Exu* across to the right shoulder, ***IN THE NAME OF EXU REI***; present the *Divine Sword of Exu* across to the right left shoulder, ***IN THE NAME OF MARIA PADILLA REINA***; and finally present the *Divine Sword of Exu* to the center of your heart in a praying position, ***SARAVA***; afterwards kiss your hands that are wraped around the handle of the *Divine Sword of Exu* three times.

After blessing yourself with the Divine Sword of Exu recite the following invocation:

Blessed are you, O Lord Nzambi, for you created the Heavens, the Earth and the Seven Quimbanda Kingdoms to protect and to serve all of mankind. Blessed are you, O Lord Nzambi, for you brought down from the heavens the Divine

Sword of Exu to triumph over and to conquer our enemies. May we worship you and give thanks to thee O powerful King of the Heavens and all your divine glory. Sarava

After reciting the sacred invocation, do the following: Stand up facing the altar of the Quimbanda Trinity in the East and hold the Divine Sword of Exu in both of your hands and point it towards the altar and towards the Heavens. Afterwards, take the Divine Sword of Exu using both of your hands and kiss it three times. After kissing the Divine Sword of Exu, stand up and perform *THE LICENSE TO DEPARTURE CONJURATION RITUAL.* Before doing *THE LICENSE TO DEPARTURE CONJURATION RITUAL ring the brass bell seven times in front of the altar of the Quimbanda Trinity.*

LICENSE TO DEPARTURE OF THE QUIMBANDA SPIRITS

If you have been initiated into the mysteries of the Quimbanda religious tradition and you have been presented the sacred and holy mysteries of the Quimbanda Trinity, then you will perform the following sacred ritual before *THE LICENSE TO DEPARTURE CONJURATION RITUAL*. The mysteries of the Quimbanda Trinity consist of the actual spirit mysteries which are the spirit ngangas of *Exu Maioral, Exu Rei* and *Maria Padilla Reina*. If you have these Quimbanda mysteries on your holy altar of the Quimbanda Trinity do the following;

Ritually feed the nganga of the Spirit, Exu Maioral.
Ritually feed the nganga of the Spirit, Exu Rei.
Ritually feed the nganga of the Spirit, Maria Padilla Reina.

After ritually feeding the spirits of the Quimbanda Trinity do the following: Take the sacred holy Sword of *Exu Maioral* out from his spirit nganga and then place it underneath the nganga with the pointed end of the sword pointed in an outward position. Take the sacred holy Sword of *Exu Rei* out from his spirit nganga and then place it underneath the nganga with the pointed end of the sword pointed in an outward position. Take the sacred holy Sword of *Maria Padilla Reina* out from her spirit nganga and then place it underneath the nganga with the pointed end of the sword pointed in an outward position. Blow smoke from a cigar over and into each of the three spirit ngangas three times Spray Cacahca liquor with your mouth over and into each of the three spirit ngangas three times. Using gun powder, carefully line up each of the blades of the three spirit swords from where it starts from underneath the nganga to the end of each of the points of the sacred and holy swords. Using a long metal rod with an attached a device of light and fire, ignite the gun powder on each of the three spirit blades. The gun powder is lighted from where it begins underneath the spirit nganga so it shots out towards the tip of the blade.

Ignite the gun powder in the following order:

First, the nganga of Exu Maioral.
Second, the nganga of Exu Rei.
Third, the nganga of Maria Padilla Reina.

THE LICENSE TO DEPARTURE CONJURATION RITUAL

A License to Depart is a simple banishing ritual that you will perform to rid the area of any astral entities and spirits that might have been attracted to you from the energies you are creating during these rituals. The License to Departure Conjuration Ritual can be done in the following ritual by reciting the following:

O Mighty God Nzambi, you are the Creator of the Heavens and the Earth. O Mighty God Nzambi you are the great force of all that is seen and unseen. O Mighty God Nzambi, by the power invested in me through thy most sacred and Holy of Holies, the Divine Sword of Exu, I do banish from this sacred ritual area any and all spirits, beings and astral entities of any kind whom have been summoned and gathered here today to assist me in this hloy ritual of Divine Justice. O Mighty God Nzambi, by the mighty Sword of Exu, the Divine Sword of the King of Kings, I grant you the license to depart, so now return to the realm of God and be on your way. In the name of Nzambi, the Lord of Heaven, in the name of the Quimbanada Trinity, Exu Maioral, Exu Rei, Maria Padilla Reina and the spirits of the Seven Greater Quimbanda Kingdoms and the spirits of the Seven Lesser Quimbanda Kingdoms, I will this to be done. O Mighty God Nzambi, Thy Kingdom come, Thy will be done on Earth as it is in the great Heavens. SARAVA

THE GREATER BANISHING RITUAL OF THE QUIMBANDA CROSS

After the License to Departure Conjuration Ritual, you must perform the banishing ritual of the Quimbanda Cross to unlock and banish the magic circle. The Greater Banishing Ritual of the Quimbanda Cross is done in a counter clockwise position. Facing East towards the altar of the Quimbanda Trinity, with the *Divine Sword of Exu* in your right hand do the following: Trace the Greater Banishing Ritual of the Quimbanda before you in the air using the Sword of Exu in silence. Turn towards the North with the *Divine Sword of Exu* in your right hand do the following: Trace the Greater Banishing Ritual of the Quimbanda before you in the air using the *Divine Sword of Exu* in silence. Turn towards the West with the *Divine Sword of Exu* in your right hand do the following: Trace the Greater Banishing Ritual of the Quimbanda before you in the air using the *Divine Sword of Exu* in silence. Turn towards the South with the *Divine Sword of Exu* in your right hand do the following: Trace the Greater Banishing Ritual of the Quimbanda before you in the air using the *Divine Sword of Exu* in silence. Turn towards the East facing the altar of the Quimbanda Trinity, with the *Divine Sword of Exu* in your right hand and say the following: *In the name of Nzambi, the Lord of Heaven - SARAVA In the name of the Quimbanda Trinity, who govern the Heavens and the Earth – SARAVA Exu by the Divine Sword of the King of Kings I lay down my enemies at your feet – SARAVA Exu by the Divine Sword of the King of Kings I do bind my enemies in thy most sacred and Holy name – SARAVA Exu by the Divine Sword of the King of Kings, I do blind my enemies in thy most sacred and Holy name – SARAVA. Exu by the Divine Sword of the King of Kings, I do destroy my enemies in thy most sacred and Holy name – SARAVA. Exu by the Divine Sword of the King of Kings, give me victory to triumph over my enemies – SARAVA. Exu by the Divine Sword of the King of Kings, give me victory to defeat my enemies – SARAVA. Exu by the Divine Sword of the King of Kings, I wash my hands clean like Pontius Pilate - SARAVA*

THE EXTINGUISHING OF THE SACRED LIGHTS OF FIRE

After the conclusion of the sacred ritual of the *Divine Sword of Exu* you must perform the sacred ceremony of the extinguishing of the sacred lights of fire in the following ritual manner. The sacred ritual candles used during the ritual of the Divine Sword of Exu should never be blown out. The candles should always be put out by using a candle snuffer.

1st - Number **4** Candle
2nd - Number **6** Candle
3rd - Number **5** Candle
4th - Number **1** Candle
5th - Number **3** Candle
6th - Number **2** Candle
7th - Number **7** Candle

THE QUIMBANDA RITUAL CLEANSING BATH

After the conclusion of performing the sacred ritual of the *Divine Sword of Exu* you must bathe yourself in a ritual bath. The ritual bath is the same as the one used at the beginning before the starting of the ritual.

SPIRIT SIGNATURE OF THE QUIMBANDA CROSS

SPIRIT SIGNATURE OF EXU MAIORAL

SPIRIT SIGNATURE OF EXU REI

SPIRIT SIGNATURE OF MARIA PADILLA POMBA GIRA

SPIRITUAL OIL

www.ingramcontent.com/pod-product-compliance
Ingram Content Group UK Ltd.
Pitfield, Milton Keynes, MK11 3LW, UK
UKHW040559210726
13854UKWH00008B/1544

9 781105 799600